Who's Buying

for Travel

7th EDITION

New Strategist Publications, Inc.
P.O. Box 242, Ithaca, New York 14851
800/848-0842; 607/273-0913
www.newstrategist.com

ISBN 978-1-935775-11-9

Printed in the United States of America

Contents

Household Spending on Travel by Product Category, 2008

About the Data in Who's Buying for Travel

Introduction

The spending data in *Who's Buying for Travel* are based on the Bureau of Labor Statistics' Consumer Expenditure Survey, an ongoing, nationwide survey of household spending. The Consumer Expenditure Survey is a complete accounting of household expenditures. It includes everything from big-ticket items, such as homes and cars, to small purchases like laundry detergent and videos. The survey does not include expenditures by government, business, or institutions. The lag time between data collection and dissemination is about two years. The data in this report are from the 2008 Consumer Expenditure Survey, unless otherwise noted.

To produce this report, New Strategist Publications analyzed the Consumer Expenditure Survey's average household spending data in a variety of ways, calculating household spending indexes, aggregate (or total) household spending, and market shares. This report shows spending data by age, household income, household type, race, Hispanic origin, region of residence, and education. These analyses are presented in two formats—for all product categories by demographic characteristic and for all demographic characteristics by product category.

Definition of consumer unit

The Consumer Expenditure Survey uses the consumer unit rather than the household as the sampling unit. The term household is used interchangeably with the term consumer unit in this report for convenience, although they are not exactly the same. Some households contain more than one consumer unit.

The Bureau of Labor Statistics defines consumer units as either: (1) members of a household who are related by blood, marriage, adoption, or other legal arrangements; (2) a person living alone or sharing a household with others or living as a roomer in a private home or lodging house or in permanent living quarters in a hotel or motel, but who is financially independent; or (3) two or more persons living together who pool their income to make joint expenditure decisions. The bureau defines financial independence in terms of the three major expense categories: housing, food, and other living expenses. To be considered financially independent, at least two of the three major expense categories have to be provided by the respondent.

The Census Bureau uses the household as its sampling unit in the decennial census and in the monthly Current Population Survey. The Census Bureau's household consists of all persons who occupy a housing unit. A house, an apartment or other groups of rooms, or a single room is regarded as a housing unit when it is occupied or intended for occupancy as separate living quarters; that is, when the occupants do not live and eat with any other persons in the structure and there is direct access from the outside or through a common hall.

The definition goes on to specify that a household includes the related family members and all the unrelated persons, if any, such as lodgers, foster children, wards, or employees who share the housing unit. A person living alone in a housing unit or a group of unrelated persons sharing a housing unit as partners is also counted as a household. The count of households excludes group quarters.

Because there can be more than one consumer unit in a household, consumer units outnumber households by several million. Young adults under age 25 head most of the additional consumer units.

How to use the tables in this report

The starting point for all calculations are the unpublished, detailed average household spending data collected by the Consumer Expenditure Survey. These numbers are shown on the report's average spending tables and on each of the product-specific tables. New Strategist's editors calculated the other figures in the report based on the average figures. The indexed spending tables and the indexed spending column (Best Customers) on the product-specific tables reveal whether spending by households in a given segment is above or below the average for all households and by how much. The total (or aggregate) spending tables show the overall size of the market. The market share tables and market share column (Biggest Customers) on the product-specific tables reveal how much spending each household segment controls. These analyses are described in detail below.

• **Average Spending** The average spending figures show the average annual spending of households on travel in 2008. The Consumer Expenditure Survey produces average spending data for all households in a segment, e.g., all households with a householder aged 25 to 34, not just for those who purchased the item. When examining spending data, it is important to remember that by including both travelers and nontravelers in the calculation, the average is less than the amount spent on the item by buyers. (See Table 1 for the percentage of households spending on travel in 2008 and how much the purchasers spent.)

Because average spending figures include both buyers and nonbuyers, they reveal spending patterns by demographic characteristic. By knowing who is most likely to spend on an item, marketers can target their advertising and promotions more efficiently, and businesses can determine the market potential of a product or service in a city or neighborhood. By multiplying the average amount households spend on airfares by the number of households in an area, for example, a newspaper could show an airline the potential size of the market in its area, convincing it to advertise to the local population.

• **Indexed Spending (Best Customers)** The indexed spending figures compare the spending of each household segment with that of the average household. To compute the indexes, New Strategist divides the average amount each household segment spends on an item by average household spending and multiplies the resulting figure by 100.

An index of 100 is the average for all households. An index of 125 means the spending of a household segment is 25 percent above average (100 plus 25). An index of 75 indicates spending that is 25 percent below the average for all households (100 minus 25). Indexed spending figures identify the best customers for a product or service. Households with an index of 178 for lodging, for example, are a strong market for this service. Those with an index below 100 are a weak market.

Spending indexes can reveal hidden markets—household segments with a high propensity to buy a particular product or service but which are overshadowed by household segments that account for a larger share of the market. Householders aged 65 to 74, for example, account for 23 percent of spending on cruises, less than the 25 percent accounted for by householders aged 45 to 54. But a look at the indexed spending figures reveals that, in fact, the older householders are the better customers. They spend over twice as much as the average household on ship fares compared with only 20 percent above average spending (index of 120) by householders aged 45 to 54. Cruise line marketers can use this information to target their best customers.

Note that because of sampling errors, small differences in index values may be insignificant. But the broader patterns revealed by indexes can guide marketers to the best customers.

• **Total (Aggregate) Spending** To produce the total (aggregate) spending figures, New Strategist multiplies average spending by the number of households in a segment. The result is the dollar size of the total household market and of each market segment. All totals are shown in thousands of dollars. To convert the numbers in the total spending tables to dollars, you must append 000 to the number. For example, households headed by married couples without children at home spent over $14 billion ($14,398,703,000) on lodging in 2008.

When comparing the total spending figures in this report with total spending estimates from the Bureau of Economic Analysis, other government agencies, or trade associations, keep in mind that the Consumer Expenditure Survey includes only household spending, not spending by businesses or institutions. Sales data also differ from household spending totals because sales figures for consumer products include the value of goods sold to industries, government, and foreign markets, which may be a significant proportion of sales.

• **Market Shares (Biggest Customers)** New Strategist produces market share figures by converting total (aggregate) spending data into percentages. To calculate the percentage of total spending on an item that is controlled by each demographic segment—i.e., its market share—each segment's total spending on an item is divided by aggregate household spending on the item.

Market shares reveal the biggest customers—the demographic segments that account for the largest share of spending on a particular product or service. In 2008, for example, households headed by college graduates accounted for 63 percent of spending on airline fares, more than double their 29 percent share of consumer units. By targeting only the best-educated consumers, airlines can reach the majority of their customers. There is a danger here, however. By single-mindedly targeting the biggest customers, businesses cannot nurture potential growth markets. With competition for customers more heated than ever, targeting potential markets is increasingly important to business survival.

• **Product Specific Tables** The product-specific tables reveal at a glance the demographic character- istics of spending by individual product category. These tables show average spending, indexed spending (Best Customers), and market shares (Biggest Customers) by age, income, household type, race and Hispanic origin, region of residence, and education. If you want to see the spending pattern for an individual product at a glance, these are the tables for you.

History and methodology of the Consumer Expenditure Survey

The Consumer Expenditure Survey is an ongoing study of the day-to-day spending of American households. In taking the survey, government interviewers collect spending data on products and services as well as the amount and sources of household income, changes in saving and debt, and demographic and economic characteristics of household members. The Bureau of the Census collects data for the Consumer Expenditure Survey under contract with the Bureau of Labor Statistics, which is responsible for analysis and release of the survey data.

Since the late 19th century, the federal government has conducted expenditure surveys about every 10 years. Although the results have been used for a variety of purposes, their primary application is to track consumer prices. In 1980, the Consumer Expenditure Survey became continuous with annual release of data (and a lag time of about two years between data collection and release). The survey is used to update prices for the market basket of products and services used in calculating the Consumer Price Index.

The Consumer Expenditure Survey consists of two separate surveys: an interview survey and a diary survey. In the interview portion of the survey, respondents are asked each quarter for five consecutive quarters to report their expenditures for the previous three months. The interview survey records purchases of big-ticket items such as houses, cars, and major appliances, and recurring expenses such as insurance premiums, utility payments, and rent. The interview component covers about 95 percent of all expenditures.

The diary survey records expenditures on small, frequently purchased items during a two-week period. These detailed records include expenses for food and beverages purchased in grocery stores and at restau- rants, as well as other items such as tobacco, housekeeping supplies, nonprescription drugs, and personal care products and services. The diary survey is intended to capture expenditures respondents are likely to forget or recall incorrectly over longer periods of time.

Two separate, nationally representative samples are used for the interview and diary surveys. For the interview survey, about 7,000 consumer units are interviewed on a rotating panel basis each quarter for five consecutive quarters. Another 7,000 consumer units kept weekly diaries of spending for two consecutive weeks. Data collection is carried out in 91 areas of the country.

The Bureau of Labor Statistics reviews, audits, and cleanses the data, then weights them to reflect the number and characteristics of all U.S. consumer units. Like any sample survey, the Consumer Expenditure Survey is subject to two major types of error. Nonsampling error occurs when respondents misinterpret questions or interviewers are inconsistent in the way they ask questions or record answers. Respondents may forget items, recall expenses incorrectly, or deliberately give wrong answers. A respondent may remember how much he or she spent at the grocery store but forget the items picked up at a local convenience store. Mistakes during the various stages of data processing and refinement can also cause nonsampling error.

Sampling error occurs when a sample does not accurately represent the population it is supposed to represent. This kind of error is present in every sample-based survey and is minimized by using a proper sampling procedure. Standard error tables documenting the extent of sampling error in the Consumer Expenditure Survey are available from the Bureau of Labor Statistics at http://www.bls.gov/cex/csxstnderror.htm.

Although the Consumer Expenditure Survey is the best source of information about the spending behavior of American households, it should be treated with caution because of the above problems.

For more information

To find out more about the Consumer Expenditure Survey, contact the specialists at the Bureau of Labor Statistics at (202) 691-6900, or visit the Consumer Expenditure Survey home page at http://www.bls.gov/cex/. The web site includes news releases, technical documentation, and current and historical summary-level data. The detailed average spending data shown in this report are available from the Bureau of Labor Statistics only by special request.

For a comprehensive look at detailed household spending data for all products and services, see the 15th edition of *Household Spending: Who Spends How Much on What.* New Strategist's books are available in hardcopy or as downloads with links to the Excel version of each table. Find out more by visiting http://www.newstrategist.com or by calling 1-800-848-0842.

Table 1. Percent reporting expenditure and amount spent, average quarter, 2008

(percent of consumer units reporting expenditure and amount spent by purchasers during the average quarter, 2008)

	average quarter	
	percent reporting expenditure	**amount spent by purchasers**
Travel		
Admission to sports events on trips	8.2%	$45.36
Airline fares	9.9	867.80
Alcoholic beverages purchased on trips	11.8	85.07
Auto rental on trips	2.0	307.91
Bus fares, intercity	4.0	69.71
Gasoline on trips	20.1	179.96
Groceries on trips	10.6	115.42
Local transportation on trips	4.8	63.72
Lodging on trips	14.2	577.09
Luggage	1.4	109.57
Movie, other admissions, on trips	8.2	136.07
Parking fees on trips	3.1	48.71
Participant sports on trips	3.7	186.18
Recreation expenses on trips	7.5	78.19
Restaurants and carry-outs on trips	23.7	251.13
Ship fares	2.2	424.10
Taxi fares and limousine services on trips	4.8	37.42
Tolls on trips	6.2	17.46
Train fares, intercity	3.9	144.82

Source: Calculations by New Strategist based on the 2008 Consumer Expenditure Survey

Household Spending Trends: 2000 to 2008

Household spending has diminished because of the Great Recession. In 2008, the average household spent $50,486—6 percent more than in 2000, after adjusting for inflation. According to data collected annually by the Bureau of Labor Statistics' Consumer Expenditure Survey, household spending reached an all-time high of $51,688 in 2006 not only because of the easy money of the housing bubble, but also because the cost of necessities was climbing. Then the recession took hold. Between 2006 and 2008, spending by the average household fell 2 percent—down $1,202—as the hard times hit.

Although overall household spending was rising between 2000 and 2006, an examination of spending trends during those years reveals two opposing forces at work. On the one hand, the numbers show that some households were awash in the easy money that resulted from surging housing prices and the abuse of home equity loans. On the other hand, the cost of necessities was rising, forcing many households to trim their spending on discretionary items well before the official start of the recession.

Average household spending on housing increased by 13 percent between 2000 and 2006, after adjusting inflation. That figure includes a 24 percent rise in property taxes as well as a 21 percent rise in spending on mortgage interest as the rate of homeownership reached a record high and some families bought larger homes than they could afford. Spending on audio and visual equipment and services grew 24 percent as some spent their home equity on big-screen TVs and other electronic toys. Average household spending on household services also grew substantially during those years.

Ominously, however, the cost of necessities was climbing sharply. The average household spent 47 percent more on gasoline in 2006 than in 2000, after adjusting for inflation. Spending on utilities and heating fuels rose 17 percent during those years. Health insurance spending climbed 27 percent, and education spending increased 20 percent. The middle class was being squeezed, and consumers were cutting back. Spending on used vehicles plummeted 24 percent between 2000 and 2006, while spending on new vehicles fell 4 percent. Spending on women's clothes declined 11 percent, and spending on footwear diminished 24 percent. Despite the record high homeownership rate, spending on household furnishings and equipment fell 6 percent between 2000 and 2006.

Those who track the government's Consumer Expenditure Survey could not have been surprised by these declines or the even deeper cuts that followed. For years, spending trends have suggested that American households were struggling. Between 2006 and 2008, spending on mortgage interest fell nearly 5 percent. Cash contributions declined 13 percent. Spending on clothing and vehicles continued to plummet. Households also cut their spending on alcoholic beverages, food away from home, and furniture. American consumers are proving to be cautious spenders, with enormous consequences for our economy.

Households are being squeezed by the rising cost of necessities

(percent change in spending by the average household on selected products and services, 2000–06 and 2006–08; in 2008 dollars)

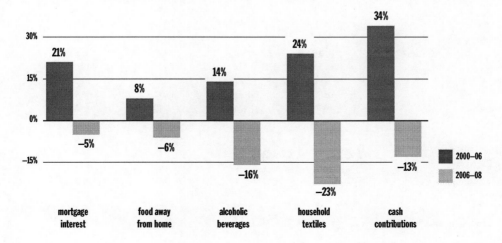

Table 2. Household spending trends, 2000 to 2008

(average annual spending of consumer units, 2000 to 2008; percent change, 2000–06, 2006–08, and 2000–08; in 2008 dollars)

	2008	2006	2000	percent change 2000–06	percent change 2006–08	percent change 2000–08
Number of consumer units (in 000s)	120,770	118,843	109,367	8.7%	1.6%	10.4%
Average annual spending of consumer units	$50,486	$51,688	$47,568	8.7	–2.3	6.1
FOOD	**6,443**	**6,526**	**6,449**	**1.2**	**–1.3**	**–0.1**
Food at home	**3,744**	**3,649**	**3,777**	**–3.4**	**2.6**	**–0.9**
Cereals and bakery products	507	476	566	–15.9	6.4	–10.5
Cereals and cereal products	170	153	195	–21.7	11.3	–12.8
Bakery products	337	325	371	–12.6	3.8	–9.2
Meats, poultry, fish, and eggs	846	851	994	–14.4	–0.6	–14.9
Beef	239	252	298	–15.3	–5.2	–19.7
Pork	163	168	209	–19.7	–2.8	–21.9
Other meats	106	112	126	–11.2	–5.5	–16.1
Poultry	159	151	181	–16.9	5.6	–12.3
Fish and seafood	128	130	138	–5.3	–1.8	–6.9
Eggs	51	40	43	–7.0	29.1	20.0
Dairy products	430	393	406	–3.3	9.4	5.8
Fresh milk and cream	168	150	164	–8.7	12.4	2.6
Other dairy products	261	243	241	0.9	7.2	8.2
Fruits and vegetables	657	632	651	–2.9	3.9	0.9
Fresh fruits	222	208	204	2.2	6.6	8.9
Fresh vegetables	212	206	199	3.7	2.9	6.6
Processed fruits	116	116	144	–19.0	–0.4	–19.3
Processed vegetables	107	101	105	–3.4	5.5	1.9
Other food at home	1,305	1,294	1,159	11.7	0.8	12.6
Sugar and other sweets	129	133	146	–8.7	–3.4	–11.8
Fats and oils	104	92	104	–11.5	13.2	0.2
Miscellaneous foods	680	670	546	22.6	1.6	24.5
Nonalcoholic beverages	342	355	313	13.4	–3.5	9.4
Food prepared by consumer unit on trips	49	46	50	–8.2	6.7	–2.0
Food away from home	**2,698**	**2,877**	**2,672**	**7.7**	**–6.2**	**1.0**
ALCOHOLIC BEVERAGES	**444**	**531**	**465**	**14.1**	**–16.3**	**–4.5**
HOUSING	**17,109**	**17,478**	**15,403**	**13.5**	**–2.1**	**11.1**
Shelter	**10,183**	**10,330**	**8,895**	**16.1**	**–1.4**	**14.5**
Owned dwellings	6,760	6,959	5,754	20.9	–2.9	17.5
Mortgage interest and charges	3,826	4,008	3,300	21.5	–4.5	16.0
Property taxes	1,758	1,761	1,424	23.7	–0.2	23.4
Maintenance, repair, insurance, other expenses	1,176	1,191	1,032	15.4	–1.2	14.0
Rented dwellings	2,724	2,766	2,543	8.8	–1.5	7.1
Other lodging	698	606	598	1.3	15.3	16.8
Utilities, fuels, and public services	**3,649**	**3,628**	**3,112**	**16.6**	**0.6**	**17.3**
Natural gas	531	544	384	41.6	–2.3	38.3
Electricity	1,353	1,352	1,139	18.7	0.1	18.8
Fuel oil and other fuels	192	147	121	21.5	30.3	58.3
Telephone services	1,127	1,161	1,097	5.9	–2.9	2.8
Water and other public services	446	424	370	14.6	5.2	20.5
Household services	**998**	**1,012**	**855**	**18.4**	**–1.4**	**16.7**
Personal services	383	420	408	3.0	–8.7	–6.0
Other household services	614	593	448	32.4	3.6	37.2
Housekeeping supplies	**654**	**684**	**603**	**13.4**	**–4.3**	**8.5**
Laundry and cleaning supplies	148	161	164	–1.5	–8.2	–9.6
Other household products	350	352	283	24.7	–0.7	23.9
Postage and stationery	156	170	158	7.8	–8.1	–1.0
Household furnishings and equipment	**1,624**	**1,824**	**1,937**	**–5.8**	**–11.0**	**–16.1**
Household textiles	126	164	133	24.1	–23.4	–4.9

	2008	2006	2000	percent change 2000–06	percent change 2006–08	percent change 2000–08
Furniture	$388	$494	$489	1.1%	−21.5%	−20.6%
Floor coverings	45	51	55	−6.8	−12.2	−18.2
Major appliances	204	257	236	8.9	−20.7	−13.7
Small appliances and miscellaneous housewares	113	116	109	7.0	−2.9	3.9
Miscellaneous household equipment	749	740	914	−19.0	1.2	−18.1
APPAREL AND RELATED SERVICES	**1,801**	**2,001**	**2,321**	**−13.8**	**−10.0**	**−22.4**
Men and boys	**427**	**474**	**550**	**−13.8**	**−9.9**	**−22.4**
Men, aged 16 or older	344	377	430	−12.3	−8.8	−20.0
Boys, aged 2 to 15	83	97	120	−19.0	−14.6	−30.9
Women and girls	**718**	**802**	**906**	**−11.5**	**−10.5**	**−20.8**
Women, aged 16 or older	597	672	759	−11.5	−11.1	−21.3
Girls, aged 2 to 15	121	130	148	−11.7	−7.1	−18.0
Children under age 2	**93**	**103**	**103**	**0.0**	**−9.3**	**−9.3**
Footwear	**314**	**325**	**429**	**−24.3**	**−3.3**	**−26.8**
Other apparel products and services	**248**	**299**	**333**	**−10.1**	**−17.1**	**−25.4**
TRANSPORTATION	**8,604**	**9,086**	**9,274**	**−2.0**	**−5.3**	**−7.2**
Vehicle purchases	**2,755**	**3,654**	**4,274**	**−14.5**	**−24.6**	**−35.5**
Cars and trucks, new	1,305	1,920	2,007	−4.3	−32.0	−35.0
Cars and trucks, used	1,315	1,675	2,213	−24.3	−21.5	−40.6
Other vehicles	134	58	54	7.3	132.4	149.2
Gasoline and motor oil	**2,715**	**2,378**	**1,614**	**47.3**	**14.2**	**68.2**
Other vehicle expenses	2,621	2,515	2,852	−11.8	4.2	−8.1
Vehicle finance charges	312	318	410	−22.4	−2.0	−23.9
Maintenance and repairs	731	735	780	−5.8	−0.5	−6.3
Vehicle insurance	1,113	946	973	−2.7	17.6	14.4
Vehicle rentals, leases, licenses, other charges	465	515	689	−25.3	−9.7	−32.5
Public transportation	**513**	**539**	**534**	**1.0**	**−4.9**	**−3.9**
HEALTH CARE	**2,976**	**2,954**	**2,583**	**14.4**	**0.7**	**15.2**
Health insurance	1,653	1,565	1,229	27.3	5.7	34.5
Medical services	727	716	710	0.8	1.6	2.4
Drugs	482	549	520	5.5	−12.2	−7.3
Medical supplies	114	125	124	0.9	−8.8	−7.9
ENTERTAINMENT	**2,835**	**2,537**	**2,329**	**8.9**	**11.7**	**21.7**
Fees and admissions	616	647	644	0.5	−4.8	−4.3
Audio and visual equipment and services	1,036	968	778	24.4	7.1	33.2
Pets, toys, and playground equipment	704	440	418	5.4	60.0	68.6
Other entertainment products and services	479	482	491	−2.0	−0.6	−2.5
PERSONAL CARE PRODUCTS AND SERVICES	**616**	**625**	**705**	**−11.4**	**−1.4**	**−12.6**
READING	**116**	**125**	**183**	**−31.5**	**−7.2**	**−36.5**
EDUCATION	**1,046**	**948**	**790**	**20.0**	**10.3**	**32.4**
TOBACCO PRODUCTS AND SMOKING SUPPLIES	**317**	**349**	**399**	**−12.4**	**−9.2**	**−20.5**
MISCELLANEOUS	**840**	**904**	**970**	**−6.9**	**−7.0**	**−13.4**
CASH CONTRIBUTIONS	**1,737**	**1,996**	**1,490**	**33.9**	**−13.0**	**16.5**
PERSONAL INSURANCE AND PENSIONS	**5,605**	**5,628**	**4,207**	**33.8**	**−0.4**	**33.2**
Life and other personal insurance	317	344	499	−31.1	−7.8	−36.5
Pensions and Social Security	5,288	5,284	–	–	–	–
PERSONAL TAXES	**1,789**	**2,597**	**3,897**	**−33.4**	**−31.1**	**−54.1**
Federal income taxes	1,817	1,827	3,012	−39.3	−0.6	−39.7
2008 tax stimulus	−784	–	–	–	–	–
State and local income taxes	542	554	703	−21.1	−2.2	−22.9
Other taxes	213	216	183	18.2	−1.3	16.7
GIFTS FOR PEOPLE IN OTHER HOUSEHOLDS	**1,209**	**1,232**	**1,354**	**−9.0**	**−1.9**	**−10.7**

Note: Spending by category does not add to total spending because gift spending is also included in the preceding product and service categories and personal taxes are not included in the total. "–" means data are unavailable.
Source: Bureau of Labor Statistics, 2000, 2006, and 2008 Consumer Expenditure Surveys, Internet site http://www.bls.gov/cex/; calculations by New Strategist

Household Spending on Travel, 2008

Travel is one of the most popular leisure-time activities of Americans. In 2008, the average household spent $1,418 on travel, including airline fares, lodging, luggage, meals, and recreational expenses. The three largest travel expense categories—airline fares, lodging, and restaurant meals—account for 64 percent of travel spending. Gasoline ranks fourth and accounts for another 10 percent of the total.

Average household spending on travel fell by 5 percent between 2000 and 2008, after adjusting for inflation. Average household spending on gasoline while traveling increased 26 percent, spending on luggage rose 20 percent, and spending on parking fees and tolls on trips climbed 9 percent. Spending declined substantially on several travel items including intercity bus fares (down 45 percent), vehicle rentals (down 38 percent), recreational expenses (down 26 percent), and ship fares (down 17 percent).

Spending by age

The best customers of travel are older Americans. Householders aged 55 to 64 spend the most on travel—34 percent more than the average household. Householders aged 45 to 54 also spend significantly more than the average household on travel. Householders aged 65 to 74 spend the most on bus and ship fares.

Spending by household income

Not surprisingly, high-income households spend far more than the average household on travel. Households with incomes of $100,000 or more accounted for 49 percent of travel spending in 2008—almost three times their 18 percent share of households. High-income households spend more than the average household on every travel category. The gap is smallest for luggage and gasoline on trips.

Spending by household type

By household type, the biggest spenders on travel are married couples without children at home, most of them empty-nesters. This household type spends 56 percent more than average on travel. Couples with school-aged or older children at home also spend more than average on travel and account for 30 percent of total travel spending. Single parents and people who live alone spend about half the average amount on travel.

Spending by race and Hispanic origin

Asians, who have higher incomes than any other racial or ethnic group, are by far the biggest spenders on travel. Asians spend 47 percent more than the average household on travel. In contrast, black and Hispanic households spend significantly less than average. Asians spend more than average in all travel categories except gas, alcohol, and lodging. Their spending on airline fares is more than two-and-one-half times the average.

Spending by region

Households in the West spend the most on travel—33 percent more than the average household. Households in the South spend 22 percent less than average on travel, the least among regions. Households in the West spend more than average on all the travel categories except parking and tolls on trips. They spend 60 percent more on vehicle rentals, 53 percent more on airfares, and 50 percent more on ship fares. Households in the Northeast spend nearly twice as much as those in other regions on parking fees and tolls while on trips.

Spending by education

Travel spending rises with educational attainment because income rises with education. College graduates account for only 29 percent of the population but for 56 percent of travel spending. They account for the majority of spending in most travel categories, including 63 percent of vehicle rentals and airfares, 60 percent of train fares and local transportation on trips, and 58 percent of ship fares. The share of travel spending controlled by college graduates is lowest for gasoline on trips.

Table 3. Travel spending, 2000 to 2008

(average annual household spending on travel, and percent distribution of spending by type, 2000 and 2008; percent change in spending, 2000–08; in 2008 dollars; ranked by amount spent)

	2008		2000		
	average household spending	percent distribution	average household spending (in 2008$)	percent distribution	percent change 2000–08
Average household spending on travel	**$1,417.96**	**100.0%**	**$1,493.56**	**100.0%**	**–5.1%**
Airline fares	343.30	24.2	342.61	22.9	0.2
Lodging on trips	328.71	23.2	314.60	21.1	4.5
Restaurant and carry-out food on trips	237.87	16.8	270.14	18.1	–11.9
Gasoline on trips	144.54	10.2	114.77	7.7	25.9
Recreational expenses on trips	134.38	9.5	182.48	12.2	–26.4
Groceries on trips	48.80	3.4	49.94	3.3	–2.3
Alcoholic beverages on trips	40.05	2.8	42.81	2.9	–6.4
Ship fares	37.83	2.7	45.74	3.1	–17.3
Vehicle rentals on trips	26.72	1.9	42.92	2.9	–37.7
Train fares, intercity	22.36	1.6	26.41	1.8	–15.3
Taxis and local transportation on trips	19.54	1.4	21.16	1.4	–7.6
Luggage	12.44	0.9	10.40	0.7	19.6
Bus fares, intercity	11.07	0.8	20.13	1.3	–45.0
Parking fees and tolls on trips	10.35	0.7	9.45	0.6	9.5

Source: Bureau of Labor Statistics, 2000 and 2008 Consumer Expenditure Surveys; calculations by New Strategist

Table 4. Travel: Average spending by age, 2008

(average annual spending of consumer units (CU) on travel, by age of consumer unit reference person, 2008)

	total consumer units	under 25	25 to 34	35 to 44	45 to 54	55 to 64	65 to 74	75+
Number of consumer units (in 000s)	120,770	8,227	20,208	22,834	25,614	19,826	12,580	11,481
Number of persons per CU	2.5	2.0	2.8	3.3	2.7	2.1	1.8	1.5
Average before-tax income of CU	$63,563.00	$28,127.00	$59,878.00	$77,582.00	$81,844.00	$71,653.00	$45,232.00	$32,886.00
Average spending of CU, total	50,485.67	29,324.54	48,159.04	58,808.25	61,178.63	54,782.72	41,433.10	31,692.05
Travel	**1,417.96**	**479.32**	**1,041.25**	**1,494.40**	**1,807.39**	**1,897.58**	**1,468.40**	**849.72**
Airline fares	343.30	117.87	258.50	379.87	440.12	449.52	323.83	203.29
Alcoholic beverages purchased on trips	40.05	21.42	38.89	39.08	46.83	52.06	37.23	24.62
Bus fares, intercity	11.07	6.27	8.54	9.29	11.81	12.70	16.31	12.33
Gasoline on trips	144.54	77.74	137.22	154.87	161.59	181.14	156.24	70.71
Groceries on trips	48.80	14.97	33.78	51.12	57.30	73.66	56.77	24.26
Lodging on trips	328.71	69.49	204.96	343.27	437.15	464.77	351.32	201.66
Luggage	12.44	3.51	11.08	13.42	25.34	10.01	5.11	3.07
Parking fees and tolls on trips	10.35	4.52	8.54	10.50	13.40	13.89	9.56	5.38
Recreational expenses on trips	134.38	47.07	101.82	165.53	180.06	159.56	118.38	64.41
Restaurants and carry-outs on trips	237.87	88.45	171.42	244.63	301.80	332.26	248.33	131.37
Ship fares	37.83	6.01	15.63	24.01	45.26	46.39	84.50	44.62
Taxis and local transportation on trips	19.54	7.41	12.36	17.60	21.75	28.13	17.84	26.79
Train fares, intercity	22.36	10.36	19.13	19.51	26.66	23.20	23.21	30.35
Vehicle rental on trips	26.72	4.23	19.38	21.70	38.32	50.29	19.77	6.86

Source: Bureau of Labor Statistics, unpublished tables from the 2008 Consumer Expenditure Survey; calculations by New Strategist

Table 5. Travel: Indexed spending by age, 2008

(indexed average annual spending of consumer units (CU) on travel by age of consumer unit reference person, 2008; index definition: an index of 100 is the average for all consumer units; an index of 132 means that spending by consumer units in that group is 32 percent above the average for all consumer units; an index of 68 indicates spending that is 32 percent below the average for all consumer units)

	total consumer units	under 25	25 to 34	35 to 44	45 to 54	55 to 64	65 to 74	75+
Average spending of CU, total	$50,486	$29,325	$48,159	$58,808	$61,179	$54,783	$41,433	$31,692
Average spending of CU, index	100	58	95	116	121	109	82	63
Travel	**100**	**34**	**73**	**105**	**127**	**134**	**104**	**60**
Airline fares	100	34	75	111	128	131	94	59
Alcoholic beverages purchased on trips	100	53	97	98	117	130	93	61
Bus fares, intercity	100	57	77	84	107	115	147	111
Gasoline on trips	100	54	95	107	112	125	108	49
Groceries on trips	100	31	69	105	117	151	116	50
Lodging on trips	100	21	62	104	133	141	107	61
Luggage	100	28	89	108	204	80	41	25
Parking fees and tolls on trips	100	44	83	101	129	134	92	52
Recreational expenses on trips	100	35	76	123	134	119	88	48
Restaurants and carry-outs on trips	100	37	72	103	127	140	104	55
Ship fares	100	16	41	63	120	123	223	118
Taxis and local transportation on trips	100	38	63	90	111	144	91	137
Train fares, intercity	100	46	86	87	119	104	104	136
Vehicle rental on trips	100	16	73	81	143	188	74	26

Source: Calculations by New Strategist based on the Bureau of Labor Statistics' 2008 Consumer Expenditure Survey

Table 6. Travel: Total spending by age, 2008

(total annual spending on travel, by consumer unit (CU) age groups, 2008; consumer units and dollars in thousands)

	total consumer units	under 25	25 to 34	35 to 44	45 to 54	55 to 64	65 to 74	75+
Number of consumer units	120,770	8,227	20,208	22,834	25,614	19,826	12,580	11,481
Total spending of all CUs	$6,097,154,366	$241,252,991	$973,197,880	$1,342,827,581	$1,567,029,429	$1,086,122,207	$521,228,398	$363,856,426
Travel	**171,247,029**	**3,943,366**	**21,041,580**	**34,123,130**	**46,294,487**	**37,621,421**	**18,472,472**	**9,755,635**
Airline fares	41,460,341	969,716	5,223,768	8,673,952	11,273,234	8,912,184	4,073,781	2,333,972
Alcoholic beverages purchased on trips	4,836,839	176,222	785,889	892,353	1,199,504	1,032,142	468,353	282,662
Bus fares, intercity	1,336,924	51,583	172,576	212,128	302,501	251,790	205,180	141,561
Gasoline on trips	17,456,096	639,567	2,772,942	3,536,302	4,138,966	3,591,282	1,965,499	811,822
Groceries on trips	5,893,576	123,158	682,626	1,167,274	1,467,682	1,460,383	714,167	278,529
Lodging on trips	39,698,307	571,694	4,141,832	7,838,227	11,197,160	9,214,530	4,419,606	2,315,258
Luggage	1,502,379	28,877	223,905	306,432	649,059	198,458	64,284	35,247
Parking fees and tolls on trips	1,249,970	37,186	172,576	239,757	343,228	275,383	120,265	61,768
Recreational expenses on trips	16,229,073	387,245	2,057,579	3,779,712	4,612,057	3,163,437	1,489,220	739,491
Restaurants and carry-outs on trips	28,727,560	727,678	3,464,055	5,585,881	7,730,305	6,587,387	3,123,991	1,508,259
Ship fares	4,568,729	49,444	315,851	548,244	1,159,290	919,728	1,063,010	512,282
Taxis and local transportation on trips	2,359,846	60,962	249,771	401,878	557,105	557,705	224,427	307,576
Train fares, intercity	2,700,417	85,232	386,579	445,491	682,869	459,963	291,982	348,448
Vehicle rental on trips	3,226,974	34,800	391,631	495,498	981,528	997,050	248,707	78,760

Note: Numbers may not add to total because of rounding.
Source: Calculations by New Strategist based on the Bureau of Labor Statistics' 2008 Consumer Expenditure Survey

Table 7. Travel: Market shares by age, 2008

(percentage of total annual spending on travel accounted for by consumer unit age groups, 2008)

	total consumer units	under 25	25 to 34	35 to 44	45 to 54	55 to 64	65 to 74	75+
Share of total consumer units	**100.0%**	**6.8%**	**16.7%**	**18.9%**	**21.2%**	**16.4%**	**10.4%**	**9.5%**
Share of total before-tax income	**100.0**	**3.0**	**15.8**	**23.1**	**27.3**	**18.5**	**7.4**	**4.9**
Share of total spending	**100.0**	**4.0**	**16.0**	**22.0**	**25.7**	**17.8**	**8.5**	**6.0**
Travel	**100.0**	**2.3**	**12.3**	**19.9**	**27.0**	**22.0**	**10.8**	**5.7**
Airline fares	100.0	2.3	12.6	20.9	27.2	21.5	9.8	5.6
Alcoholic beverages purchased on trips	100.0	3.6	16.2	18.4	24.8	21.3	9.7	5.8
Bus fares, intercity	100.0	3.9	12.9	15.9	22.6	18.8	15.3	10.6
Gasoline on trips	100.0	3.7	15.9	20.3	23.7	20.6	11.3	4.7
Groceries on trips	100.0	2.1	11.6	19.8	24.9	24.8	12.1	4.7
Lodging on trips	100.0	1.4	10.4	19.7	28.2	23.2	11.1	5.8
Luggage	100.0	1.9	14.9	20.4	43.2	13.2	4.3	2.3
Parking fees and tolls on trips	100.0	3.0	13.8	19.2	27.5	22.0	9.6	4.9
Recreational expenses on trips	100.0	2.4	12.7	23.3	28.4	19.5	9.2	4.6
Restaurants and carry-outs on trips	100.0	2.5	12.1	19.4	26.9	22.9	10.9	5.3
Ship fares	100.0	1.1	6.9	12.0	25.4	20.1	23.3	11.2
Taxis and local transportation on trips	100.0	2.6	10.6	17.0	23.6	23.6	9.5	13.0
Train fares, intercity	100.0	3.2	14.3	16.5	25.3	17.0	10.8	12.9
Vehicle rental on trips	100.0	1.1	12.1	15.4	30.4	30.9	7.7	2.4

Note: Numbers may not add to total because of rounding.
Source: Calculations by New Strategist based on the Bureau of Labor Statistics' 2008 Consumer Expenditure Survey

Table 8. Travel: Average spending by income, 2008

(average annual spending on travel, by before-tax income of consumer units (CU), 2008)

	total consumer units	under $20,000	$20,000–$39,999	$40,000–$49,999	$50,000–$69,999	$70,000–$79,999	$80,000–$99,999	$100,000 or more
Number of consumer units (in 000s)	120,770	25,311	26,898	11,287	18,287	7,354	10,017	21,615
Number of persons per CU	2.5	1.7	2.2	2.5	2.7	2.9	3.0	3.2
Average before-tax income of CU	$63,563.00	$10,699.58	$29,345.65	$44,733.00	$59,319.00	$74,486.00	$88,839.00	$166,035.00
Average spending of CU, total	50,485.67	22,367.46	32,820.58	40,526.81	50,464.69	58,742.08	67,179.65	100,065.29
Travel	**1,417.96**	**410.55**	**627.39**	**823.61**	**1,132.44**	**1,523.21**	**1,889.92**	**3,878.48**
Airline fares	343.30	99.45	138.81	161.86	270.85	345.34	420.63	1,002.84
Alcoholic beverages purchased on trips	40.05	10.94	16.95	26.45	29.14	34.02	50.85	116.29
Bus fares, intercity	11.07	5.86	8.28	7.21	8.34	8.51	11.56	25.64
Gasoline on trips	144.54	53.07	95.20	116.72	150.68	205.40	218.62	267.37
Groceries on trips	48.80	16.59	28.65	34.82	44.93	55.22	74.46	108.10
Lodging on trips	328.71	76.90	129.12	187.49	243.00	315.90	432.60	974.41
Luggage	12.44	3.64	9.47	10.90	5.73	38.92	18.71	20.44
Parking fees and tolls on trips	10.35	2.29	5.37	5.68	9.17	12.00	15.20	26.62
Recreational expenses on trips	134.38	33.72	50.25	79.77	103.00	133.34	177.20	392.54
Restaurants and carry-outs on trips	237.87	65.06	104.40	149.71	193.40	252.11	334.24	640.46
Ship fares	37.83	29.34	14.29	7.31	22.62	42.50	38.50	103.95
Taxis and local transportation on trips	19.54	3.54	6.41	9.60	13.95	21.20	30.87	58.70
Train fares, intercity	22.36	5.00	8.35	10.25	16.63	38.51	34.96	59.97
Vehicle rental on trips	26.72	5.14	11.85	15.84	21.00	20.24	31.52	81.15

Source: Bureau of Labor Statistics, unpublished tables from the 2008 Consumer Expenditure Survey; calculations by New Strategist

Table 9. Travel: Indexed spending by income, 2008

(indexed average annual spending of consumer units (CU) on travel by before-tax income of consumer unit, 2008; index definition: an index of 100 is the average for all consumer units; an index of 132 means that spending by consumer units in that group is 32 percent above the average for all consumer units; an index of 68 indicates spending that is 32 percent below the average for all consumer units)

	total consumer units	under $20,000	$20,000– $39,999	$40,000– $49,999	$50,000– $69,999	$70,000– $79,999	$80,000– $99,999	$100,000 or more
Average spending of CU, total	$50,486	$22,367	$32,821	$40,527	$50,465	$58,742	$67,180	$100,065
Average spending of CU, index	100	44	65	80	100	116	133	198
Travel	100	29	44	58	80	107	133	274
Airline fares	100	29	40	47	79	101	123	292
Alcoholic beverages purchased on trips	100	27	42	66	73	85	127	290
Bus fares, intercity	100	53	75	65	75	77	104	232
Gasoline on trips	100	37	66	81	104	142	151	185
Groceries on trips	100	34	59	71	92	113	153	222
Lodging on trips	100	23	39	57	74	96	132	296
Luggage	100	29	76	88	46	313	150	164
Parking fees and tolls on trips	100	22	52	55	89	116	147	257
Recreational expenses on trips	100	25	37	59	77	99	132	292
Restaurants and carry-outs on trips	100	27	44	63	81	106	141	269
Ship fares	100	78	38	19	60	112	102	275
Taxis and local transportation on trips	100	18	33	49	71	108	158	300
Train fares, intercity	100	22	37	46	74	172	156	268
Vehicle rental on trips	100	19	44	59	79	76	118	304

Source: Calculations by New Strategist based on the Bureau of Labor Statistics' 2008 Consumer Expenditure Survey

Table 10. Travel: Total spending by income, 2008

(total annual spending on travel, by before-tax income group of consumer units (CU), 2008; consumer units and dollars in thousands)

	total consumer units	under $20,000	$20,000– $39,999	$40,000– $49,999	$50,000– $69,999	$70,000– $79,999	$80,000– $99,999	$100,000 or more
Number of consumer units	120,770	25,311	26,898	11,287	18,287	7,354	10,017	21,615
Total spending of all CUs	$6,097,154,366	$566,142,850	$882,807,916	$457,426,104	$922,847,786	$431,989,256	$672,938,554	$2,162,911,243
Travel	171,247,029	10,391,330	16,875,544	9,296,086	20,708,930	11,201,686	18,931,329	83,833,345
Airline fares	41,460,341	2,517,232	3,733,633	1,826,914	4,953,034	2,539,630	4,213,451	21,676,387
Alcoholic beverages purchased on trips	4,836,839	276,865	455,862	298,541	532,883	250,183	509,364	2,513,608
Bus fares, intercity	1,336,924	148,289	222,750	81,379	152,514	62,583	115,797	554,209
Gasoline on trips	17,456,096	1,343,355	2,560,604	1,317,419	2,755,485	1,510,512	2,189,917	5,779,203
Groceries on trips	5,893,576	419,822	770,734	393,013	821,635	406,088	745,866	2,336,582
Lodging on trips	39,698,307	1,946,456	3,472,991	2,116,200	4,443,741	2,323,129	4,333,354	21,061,872
Luggage	1,502,379	92,092	254,622	123,028	104,785	286,218	187,418	441,811
Parking fees and tolls on trips	1,249,970	58,043	144,442	64,110	167,692	88,248	152,258	575,391
Recreational expenses on trips	16,229,073	853,602	1,351,509	900,364	1,883,561	980,582	1,775,012	8,484,752
Restaurants and carry-outs on trips	28,727,560	1,646,758	2,808,040	1,689,777	3,536,706	1,854,017	3,348,082	13,843,543
Ship fares	4,568,729	742,641	384,397	82,508	413,652	312,545	385,655	2,246,879
Taxis and local transportation on trips	2,359,846	89,658	172,498	108,355	255,104	155,905	309,225	1,268,801
Train fares, intercity	2,700,417	126,530	224,671	115,692	304,113	283,203	350,194	1,296,252
Vehicle rental on trips	3,226,974	129,986	318,792	178,786	384,027	148,845	315,736	1,754,057

Note: Numbers may not add to total because of rounding.
Source: Calculations by New Strategist based on the Bureau of Labor Statistics' 2008 Consumer Expenditure Survey

Table 11. Travel: Market shares by income, 2008

(percentage of total annual spending on travel accounted for by before-tax income group of consumer units, 2008)

	total consumer units	under $20,000	$20,000– $39,999	$40,000– $49,999	$50,000– $69,999	$70,000– $79,999	$80,000– $99,999	$100,000 or more
Share of total consumer units	100.0%	21.0%	22.3%	9.3%	15.1%	6.1%	8.3%	17.9%
Share of total before-tax income	100.0	3.5	10.3	6.6	14.1	7.1	11.6	46.8
Share of total spending	100.0	9.3	14.5	7.5	15.1	7.1	11.0	35.5
Travel	100.0	6.1	9.9	5.4	12.1	6.5	11.1	49.0
Airline fares	100.0	6.1	9.0	4.4	11.9	6.1	10.2	52.3
Alcoholic beverages purchased on trips	100.0	5.7	9.4	6.2	11.0	5.2	10.5	52.0
Bus fares, intercity	100.0	11.1	16.7	6.1	11.4	4.7	8.7	41.5
Gasoline on trips	100.0	7.7	14.7	7.5	15.8	8.7	12.5	33.1
Groceries on trips	100.0	7.1	13.1	6.7	13.9	6.9	12.7	39.6
Lodging on trips	100.0	4.9	8.7	5.3	11.2	5.9	10.9	53.1
Luggage	100.0	6.1	16.9	8.2	7.0	19.1	12.5	29.4
Parking fees and tolls on trips	100.0	4.6	11.6	5.1	13.4	7.1	12.2	46.0
Recreational expenses on trips	100.0	5.3	8.3	5.5	11.6	6.0	10.9	52.3
Restaurants and carry-outs on trips	100.0	5.7	9.8	5.9	12.3	6.5	11.7	48.2
Ship fares	100.0	16.3	8.4	1.8	9.1	6.8	8.4	49.2
Taxis and local transportation on trips	100.0	3.8	7.3	4.6	10.8	6.6	13.1	53.8
Train fares, intercity	100.0	4.7	8.3	4.3	11.3	10.5	13.0	48.0
Vehicle rental on trips	100.0	4.0	9.9	5.5	11.9	4.6	9.8	54.4

Note: Numbers may not add to total because of rounding.
Source: Calculations by New Strategist based on the Bureau of Labor Statistics' 2008 Consumer Expenditure Survey

Table 12. Travel: Average spending by high-income consumer units, 2008

(average annual spending on travel, by before-tax income of consumer units with high incomes, 2008)

	total consumer units	$100,000 or more	$100,000–$119,999	$120,000–$149,999	$150,000 or more
Number of consumer units (in 000s)	120,770	21,615	7,136	5,777	8,702
Number of persons per consumer unit	2.5	3.2	3.1	3.3	3.2
Average before-tax income of consumer units	$63,563.00	$166,035.00	$108,630.00	$132,531.00	$235,348.00
Average spending of consumer units, total	50,485.67	100,065.29	77,585.62	91,589.87	124,677.52
Travel	1,417.96	3,878.48	2,282.67	3,163.87	5,663.13
Airline fares	343.30	1,002.84	572.26	840.44	1,463.72
Alcoholic beverages purchased on trips	40.05	116.29	77.81	92.58	163.58
Bus fares, intercity	11.07	25.64	14.32	19.68	38.88
Gasoline on trips	144.54	267.37	217.72	270.68	305.89
Groceries on trips	48.80	108.10	65.02	98.73	149.65
Lodging on trips	328.71	974.41	503.78	728.73	1,523.42
Luggage	12.44	20.44	14.22	17.54	29.14
Parking fees and tolls on trips	10.35	26.62	16.06	20.12	39.60
Recreational expenses on trips	134.38	392.54	227.34	287.92	597.46
Restaurants and carry-outs on trips	237.87	640.46	398.90	547.44	900.30
Ship fares	37.83	103.95	79.18	97.28	128.68
Taxis and local transportation on trips	19.54	58.70	31.30	44.31	90.73
Train fares, intercity	22.36	59.97	27.02	42.62	98.52
Vehicle rental on trips	26.72	81.15	37.74	55.80	133.56

Source: Bureau of Labor Statistics, unpublished tables from the 2008 Consumer Expenditure Survey; calculations by New Strategist

Table 13. Travel: Indexed spending by high-income consumer units, 2008

(indexed average annual spending of consumer units with high incomes on travel, by before-tax income of consumer unit, 2008; index definition: an index of 100 is the average for all consumer units; an index of 132 means that spending by consumer units in that group is 32 percent above the average for all consumer units; an index of 68 indicates spending that is 32 percent below the average for all consumer units)

	total consumer units	$100,000 or more	$100,000– $119,999	$120,000– $149,999	$150,000 or more
Average spending of consumer units, total	$50,486	$100,065	$77,586	$91,590	$124,678
Average spending of consumer units, index	100	198	154	181	247
Travel	**100**	**274**	**161**	**223**	**399**
Airline fares	100	292	167	245	426
Alcoholic beverages purchased on trips	100	290	194	231	408
Bus fares, intercity	100	232	129	178	351
Gasoline on trips	100	185	151	187	212
Groceries on trips	100	222	133	202	307
Lodging on trips	100	296	153	222	463
Luggage	100	164	114	141	234
Parking fees and tolls on trips	100	257	155	194	383
Recreational expenses on trips	100	292	169	214	445
Restaurants and carry-outs on trips	100	269	168	230	378
Ship fares	100	275	209	257	340
Taxis and local transportation on trips	100	300	160	227	464
Train fares, intercity	100	268	121	191	441
Vehicle rental on trips	100	304	141	209	500

Source: Calculations by New Strategist based on the Bureau of Labor Statistics' 2008 Consumer Expenditure Survey

Table 14. Travel: Total spending by high-income consumer units, 2008

(total annual spending on travel, by before-tax income group of consumer units with high incomes, 2008; consumer units and dollars in thousands)

	total consumer units	$100,000 or more	$100,000– $119,999	$120,000– $149,999	$150,000 or more
Number of consumer units	120,770	21,615	7,136	5,777	8,702
Total spending of all consumer units	$6,097,154,366	$2,162,911,243	$553,650,984	$529,114,679	$1,084,943,779
Travel	171,247,029	83,833,345	16,289,133	18,277,677	49,280,557
Airline fares	41,460,341	21,676,387	4,083,647	4,855,222	12,737,291
Alcoholic beverages purchased on trips	4,836,839	2,513,608	555,252	534,835	1,423,473
Bus fares, intercity	1,336,924	554,209	102,188	113,691	338,334
Gasoline on trips	17,456,096	5,779,203	1,553,650	1,563,718	2,661,855
Groceries on trips	5,893,576	2,336,582	463,983	570,363	1,302,254
Lodging on trips	39,698,307	21,061,872	3,594,974	4,209,873	13,256,801
Luggage	1,502,379	441,811	101,474	101,329	253,576
Parking fees and tolls on trips	1,249,970	575,391	114,604	116,233	344,599
Recreational expenses on trips	16,229,073	8,484,752	1,622,298	1,663,314	5,199,097
Restaurants and carry-outs on trips	28,727,560	13,843,543	2,846,550	3,162,561	7,834,411
Ship fares	4,568,729	2,246,879	565,028	561,987	1,119,773
Taxis and local transportation on trips	2,359,846	1,268,801	223,357	255,979	789,532
Train fares, intercity	2,700,417	1,296,252	192,815	246,216	857,321
Vehicle rental on trips	3,226,974	1,754,057	269,313	322,357	1,162,239

Note: Numbers may not add to total because of rounding.
Source: Calculations by New Strategist based on the Bureau of Labor Statistics' 2008 Consumer Expenditure Survey

Table 15. Travel: Market shares by high-income consumer units, 2008

(percentage of total annual spending on travel accounted for by before-tax income group of consumer units with high incomes, 2008)

	total consumer units	$100,000 or more	$100,000–$119,999	$120,000–$149,999	$150,000 or more
Share of total consumer units	100.0%	17.9%	5.9%	4.8%	7.2%
Share of total before-tax income	100.0	46.8	10.1	10.0	26.7
Share of total spending	100.0	35.5	9.1	8.7	17.8
Travel	100.0	49.0	9.5	10.7	28.8
Airline fares	100.0	52.3	9.8	11.7	30.7
Alcoholic beverages purchased on trips	100.0	52.0	11.5	11.1	29.4
Bus fares, intercity	100.0	41.5	7.6	8.5	25.3
Gasoline on trips	100.0	33.1	8.9	9.0	15.2
Groceries on trips	100.0	39.6	7.9	9.7	22.1
Lodging on trips	100.0	53.1	9.1	10.6	33.4
Luggage	100.0	29.4	6.8	6.7	16.9
Parking fees and tolls on trips	100.0	46.0	9.2	9.3	27.6
Recreational expenses on trips	100.0	52.3	10.0	10.2	32.0
Restaurants and carry-outs on trips	100.0	48.2	9.9	11.0	27.3
Ship fares	100.0	49.2	12.4	12.3	24.5
Taxis and local transportation on trips	100.0	53.8	9.5	10.8	33.5
Train fares, intercity	100.0	48.0	7.1	9.1	31.7
Vehicle rental on trips	100.0	54.4	8.3	10.0	36.0

Note: Numbers may not add to total because of rounding.
Source: Calculations by New Strategist based on the Bureau of Labor Statistics' 2008 Consumer Expenditure Survey

Table 16. Travel: Average spending by household type, 2008

(average annual spending of consumer units (CU) on travel, by type of consumer unit, 2008)

	total consumer units	total married couples	married couples, no children	married couples with children				single parent, at least one child <18	single person
				total	oldest child under 6	oldest child 6 to 17	oldest child 18 or older		
Number of consumer units (in 000s)	120,770	61,244	26,919	29,804	5,343	15,479	8,982	6,977	35,064
Number of persons per CU	2.5	3.2	2.0	4.0	3.5	4.2	3.9	2.9	1.0
Average before-tax income of CU	$63,563.00	$85,829.00	$75,312.00	$94,697.00	$81,190.00	$97,616.00	$97,702.00	$37,100.00	$32,994.00
Average spending of CU, total	50,485.67	65,016.45	58,164.09	71,307.58	63,193.95	72,723.81	73,808.73	37,129.28	30,120.09
Travel	**1,417.96**	**2,021.93**	**2,212.35**	**1,951.48**	**1,245.51**	**2,065.89**	**2,175.19**	**783.74**	**759.24**
Airline fares	343.30	487.22	509.37	476.79	307.46	497.85	541.21	175.82	188.73
Alcoholic beverages purchased on trips	40.05	50.80	63.68	42.40	37.39	42.87	44.57	18.59	29.62
Bus fares, intercity	11.07	13.74	19.56	9.46	4.84	10.38	10.63	5.85	9.56
Gasoline on trips	144.54	203.93	214.98	200.90	162.41	222.17	187.13	84.41	76.95
Groceries on trips	48.80	69.55	75.86	67.32	50.36	71.89	69.54	26.68	24.76
Lodging on trips	328.71	480.04	534.89	464.26	246.86	504.79	523.73	186.94	166.11
Luggage	12.44	15.92	13.98	19.57	5.15	13.87	38.93	24.37	6.91
Parking fees and tolls on trips	10.35	14.72	16.71	13.78	13.06	13.97	13.89	6.77	5.44
Recreational expenses on trips	134.38	192.58	185.03	209.96	152.44	232.92	204.59	84.79	67.26
Restaurants and carry-outs on trips	237.87	339.57	372.42	328.06	201.79	351.62	362.58	123.34	125.44
Ship fares	37.83	61.02	97.68	32.06	8.90	23.61	60.39	11.06	14.04
Taxis and local transportation on trips	19.54	25.00	31.11	20.92	10.68	18.35	31.44	8.78	13.62
Train fares, intercity	22.36	30.42	35.12	28.22	15.82	27.00	37.70	15.35	15.17
Vehicle rental on trips	26.72	37.42	41.96	37.78	28.35	34.60	48.86	10.99	15.63

Source: Bureau of Labor Statistics, unpublished data from the 2008 Consumer Expenditure Survey; calculations by New Strategist

Table 17. Travel: Indexed spending by household type, 2008

(indexed average annual spending of consumer units (CU) on travel by type of consumer unit, 2008; index definition: an index of 100 is the average for all consumer units; an index of 132 means that spending by consumer units in that group is 32 percent above the average for all consumer units; an index of 68 indicates spending that is 32 percent below the average for all consumer units)

	total consumer units	total married couples	married couples, no children	married couples with children				single parent, at least one child <18	single person
				total	oldest child under 6	oldest child 6 to 17	oldest child 18 or older		
Average spending of CU, total	$50,486	$65,016	$58,164	$71,308	$63,194	$72,724	$73,809	$37,129	$30,120
Average spending of CU, index	100	129	115	141	125	144	146	74	60
Travel	**100**	**143**	**156**	**138**	**88**	**146**	**153**	**55**	**54**
Airline fares	100	142	148	139	90	145	158	51	55
Alcoholic beverages purchased on trips	100	127	159	106	93	107	111	46	74
Bus fares, intercity	100	124	177	85	44	94	96	53	86
Gasoline on trips	100	141	149	139	112	154	129	58	53
Groceries on trips	100	143	155	138	103	147	143	55	51
Lodging on trips	100	146	163	141	75	154	159	57	51
Luggage	100	128	112	157	41	111	313	196	56
Parking fees and tolls on trips	100	142	161	133	126	135	134	65	53
Recreational expenses on trips	100	143	138	156	113	173	152	63	50
Restaurants and carry-outs on trips	100	143	157	138	85	148	152	52	53
Ship fares	100	161	258	85	24	62	160	29	37
Taxis and local transportation on trips	100	128	159	107	55	94	161	45	70
Train fares, intercity	100	136	157	126	71	121	169	69	68
Vehicle rental on trips	100	140	157	141	106	129	183	41	58

tSource: Calculations by New Strategist based on the Bureau of Labor Statistics' 2008 Consumer Expenditure Survey

Table 18. Travel: Total spending by household type, 2008

(total annual spending on travel, by consumer unit (CU) type, 2008; consumer units and dollars in thousands)

| | total consumer units | total married couples | married couples, no children | married couples with children | | | | single parent, at least one child <18 | single person |
				total	oldest child under 6	oldest child 6 to 17	oldest child 18 or older		
Number of consumer units	120,770	61,244	26,919	29,804	5,343	15,479	8,982	6,977	35,064
Total spending of all CUs	$6,097,154,366	$3,981,867,464	$1,565,719,139	$2,125,251,114	$337,645,275	$1,125,691,855	$662,950,013	$259,050,987	$1,056,130,836
Travel	171,247,029	123,831,081	59,554,250	58,161,910	6,654,760	31,977,911	19,537,557	5,468,154	26,621,991
Airline fares	41,460,341	29,839,302	13,711,731	14,210,249	1,642,759	7,706,220	4,861,148	1,226,696	6,617,629
Alcoholic beverages purchased on trips	4,836,839	3,111,195	1,714,202	1,263,690	199,775	663,585	400,328	129,702	1,038,596
Bus fares, intercity	1,336,924	841,493	526,536	281,946	25,860	160,672	95,479	40,815	335,212
Gasoline on trips	17,456,096	12,489,489	5,787,047	5,987,624	867,757	3,438,969	1,680,802	588,929	2,698,175
Groceries on trips	5,893,576	4,259,520	2,042,075	2,006,405	269,073	1,112,785	624,608	186,146	868,185
Lodging on trips	39,698,307	29,399,570	14,398,704	13,836,805	1,318,973	7,813,644	4,704,143	1,304,280	5,824,481
Luggage	1,502,379	975,004	376,328	583,264	27,516	214,694	349,669	170,029	242,292
Parking fees and tolls on trips	1,249,970	901,512	449,816	410,699	69,780	216,242	124,760	47,234	190,748
Recreational expenses on trips	16,229,073	11,794,370	4,980,823	6,257,648	814,487	3,605,369	1,837,627	591,580	2,358,405
Restaurants and carry-outs on trips	28,727,560	20,796,625	10,025,174	9,777,500	1,078,164	5,442,726	3,256,694	860,543	4,398,428
Ship fares	4,568,729	3,737,109	2,629,448	955,516	47,553	365,459	542,423	77,166	492,299
Taxis and local transportation on trips	2,359,846	1,531,100	837,450	623,500	57,063	284,040	282,394	61,258	477,572
Train fares, intercity	2,700,417	1,863,042	945,395	841,069	84,526	417,933	338,621	107,097	531,921
Vehicle rental on trips	3,226,974	2,291,750	1,129,521	1,125,995	151,474	535,573	438,861	76,677	548,050

Note: Numbers do not add to total because not all types of consumer units are shown and because of rounding.
Source: Calculations by New Strategist based on the Bureau of Labor Statistics' 2008 Consumer Expenditure Survey

Table 19. Travel: Market shares by household type, 2008

(percentage of total annual spending on travel accounted for by types of consumer units, 2008)

| | total consumer units | total married couples | married couples, no children | married couples with children | | | | single parent, at least one child <18 | single person |
				total	oldest child under 6	oldest child 6 to 17	oldest child 18 or older		
Share of total consumer units	100.0%	50.7%	22.3%	24.7%	4.4%	12.8%	7.4%	5.8%	29.0%
Share of total before-tax income	100.0	68.5	26.4	36.8	5.7	19.7	11.4	3.4	15.1
Share of total spending	100.0	65.3	25.7	34.9	5.5	18.5	10.9	4.2	17.3
Travel	100.0	72.3	34.8	34.0	3.9	18.7	11.4	3.2	15.5
Airline fares	100.0	72.0	33.1	34.3	4.0	18.6	11.7	3.0	16.0
Alcoholic beverages purchased on trips	100.0	64.3	35.4	26.1	4.1	13.7	8.3	2.7	21.5
Bus fares, intercity	100.0	62.9	39.4	21.1	1.9	12.0	7.1	3.1	25.1
Gasoline on trips	100.0	71.5	33.2	34.3	5.0	19.7	9.6	3.4	15.5
Groceries on trips	100.0	72.3	34.6	34.0	4.6	18.9	10.6	3.2	14.7
Lodging on trips	100.0	74.1	36.3	34.9	3.3	19.7	11.8	3.3	14.7
Luggage	100.0	64.9	25.0	38.8	1.8	14.3	23.3	11.3	16.1
Parking fees and tolls on trips	100.0	72.1	36.0	32.9	5.6	17.3	10.0	3.8	15.3
Recreational expenses on trips	100.0	72.7	30.7	38.6	5.0	22.2	11.3	3.6	14.5
Restaurants and carry-outs on trips	100.0	72.4	34.9	34.0	3.8	18.9	11.3	3.0	15.3
Ship fares	100.0	81.8	57.6	20.9	1.0	8.0	11.9	1.7	10.8
Taxis and local transportation on trips	100.0	64.9	35.5	26.4	2.4	12.0	12.0	2.6	20.2
Train fares, intercity	100.0	69.0	35.0	31.1	3.1	15.5	12.5	4.0	19.7
Vehicle rental on trips	100.0	71.0	35.0	34.9	4.7	16.6	13.6	2.4	17.0

Note: Market shares by type of consumer unit do not add to total because not all types of consumer units are shown.
Source: Calculations by New Strategist based on the Bureau of Labor Statistics' 2008 Consumer Expenditure Survey

Table 20. Travel: Average spending by race and Hispanic origin, 2008

(average annual spending of consumer units on travel, by race and Hispanic origin of consumer unit reference person, 2008)

	total consumer units	Asian	black	Hispanic	non-Hispanic white and other
Number of consumer units (in 000s)	120,770	4,609	14,832	13,975	92,214
Number of persons per consumer unit	2.5	2.7	2.5	3.2	2.4
Average before-tax income of consumer units	$63,563.00	$75,917.00	$43,722.00	$49,317.00	$68,842.00
Average spending of consumer units, total	50,485.67	55,430.23	36,721.21	43,052.49	53,772.69
Travel	**1,417.96**	**2,085.82**	**456.52**	**854.08**	**1,655.10**
Airline fares	343.30	921.35	120.15	223.89	396.44
Alcoholic beverages purchased on trips	40.05	27.83	9.22	24.99	47.21
Bus fares, intercity	11.07	23.08	6.42	9.64	12.06
Gasoline on trips	144.54	111.90	53.11	101.24	165.59
Groceries on trips	48.80	48.81	13.91	35.88	56.32
Lodging on trips	328.71	301.06	106.66	141.38	392.06
Luggage	12.44	35.21	2.16	4.17	15.21
Parking fees and tolls on trips	10.35	12.60	4.07	6.58	11.94
Recreational expenses on trips	134.38	172.43	32.20	103.82	155.11
Restaurants and carry-outs on trips	237.87	288.05	75.01	148.29	277.24
Ship fares	37.83	55.92	8.26	10.26	46.70
Taxis and local transportation on trips	19.54	25.76	6.29	17.73	21.92
Train fares, intercity	22.36	27.62	7.00	12.41	26.28
Vehicle rental on trips	26.72	34.20	12.06	13.80	31.02

Note: "Asian" and "black" include Hispanics and non-Hispanics who identify themselves as being of the respective race alone. "Hispanic" includes people of any race who identify themselves as Hispanic. "Other" includes people who identify themselves as non-Hispanic and as Alaska Native, American Indian, Asian (who are also included in the Asian column), Native Hawaiian or other Pacific Islander, as well as non-Hispanics reporting more than one race.
Source: Bureau of Labor Statistics, unpublished tables from the 2008 Consumer Expenditure Survey; calculations by New Strategist

Table 21. Travel: Indexed spending by race and Hispanic origin, 2008

(indexed average annual spending of consumer units on travel by race and Hispanic origin of consumer unit reference person, 2008; index definition: an index of 100 is the average for all consumer units; an index of 132 means that spending by consumer units in that group is 32 percent above the average for all consumer units; an index of 68 indicates spending that is 32 percent below the average for all consumer units)

	total consumer units	Asian	black	Hispanic	non-Hispanic white and other
Average spending of consumer units, total	$50,486	$55,430	$36,721	$43,052	$53,773
Average spending of consumer units, index	100	110	73	85	107
Travel	100	147	32	60	117
Airline fares	100	268	35	65	115
Alcoholic beverages purchased on trips	100	69	23	62	118
Bus fares, intercity	100	208	58	87	109
Gasoline on trips	100	77	37	70	115
Groceries on trips	100	100	29	74	115
Lodging on trips	100	92	32	43	119
Luggage	100	283	17	34	122
Parking fees and tolls on trips	100	122	39	64	115
Recreational expenses on trips	100	128	24	77	115
Restaurants and carry-outs on trips	100	121	32	62	117
Ship fares	100	148	22	27	123
Taxis and local transportation on trips	100	132	32	91	112
Train fares, intercity	100	124	31	56	118
Vehicle rental on trips	100	128	45	52	116

Note: "Asian" and "black" include Hispanics and non-Hispanics who identify themselves as being of the respective race alone. "Hispanic" includes people of any race who identify themselves as Hispanic. "Other" includes people who identify themselves as non-Hispanic and as Alaska Native, American Indian, Asian (who are also included in the Asian column), Native Hawaiian or other Pacific Islander, as well as non-Hispanics reporting more than one race.
Source: Calculations by New Strategist based on the Bureau of Labor Statistics' 2008 Consumer Expenditure Survey

Table 22. Travel: Total spending by race and Hispanic origin, 2008

(total annual spending on travel, by consumer unit race and Hispanic origin groups, 2008; consumer units and dollars in thousands)

	total consumer units	Asian	black	Hispanic	non-Hispanic white and other
Number of consumer units	120,770	4,609	14,832	13,975	92,214
Total spending of all consumer units	$6,097,154,366	$255,477,930	$544,648,987	$601,658,548	$4,958,594,836
Travel	171,247,029	9,613,544	6,771,105	11,935,768	152,623,391
Airline fares	41,460,341	4,246,502	1,782,065	3,128,863	36,557,318
Alcoholic beverages purchased on trips	4,836,839	128,268	136,751	349,235	4,353,423
Bus fares, intercity	1,336,924	106,376	95,221	134,719	1,112,101
Gasoline on trips	17,456,096	515,747	787,728	1,414,829	15,269,716
Groceries on trips	5,893,576	224,965	206,313	501,423	5,193,492
Lodging on trips	39,698,307	1,387,586	1,581,981	1,975,786	36,153,421
Luggage	1,502,379	162,283	32,037	58,276	1,402,575
Parking fees and tolls on trips	1,249,970	58,073	60,366	91,956	1,101,035
Recreational expenses on trips	16,229,073	794,730	477,590	1,450,885	14,303,314
Restaurants and carry-outs on trips	28,727,560	1,327,622	1,112,548	2,072,353	25,565,409
Ship fares	4,568,729	257,735	122,512	143,384	4,306,394
Taxis and local transportation on trips	2,359,846	118,728	93,293	247,777	2,021,331
Train fares, intercity	2,700,417	127,301	103,824	173,430	2,423,384
Vehicle rental on trips	3,226,974	157,628	178,874	192,855	2,860,478

Note: "Asian" and "black" include Hispanics and non-Hispanics who identify themselves as being of the respective race alone. "Hispanic" includes people of any race who identify themselves as Hispanic. "Other" includes people who identify themselves as non-Hispanic and as Alaska Native, American Indian, Asian (who are also included in the Asian column), Native Hawaiian or other Pacific Islander, as well as non-Hispanics reporting more than one race. Numbers may not add to total because of rounding.
Source: Calculations by New Strategist based on the Bureau of Labor Statistics' 2008 Consumer Expenditure Survey

Table 23. Travel: Market shares by race and Hispanic origin, 2008

(percentage of total annual spending on travel accounted for by consumer unit race and Hispanic origin groups, 2008)

	total consumer units	Asian	black	Hispanic	non-Hispanic white and other
Share of total consumer units	100.0%	3.8%	12.3%	11.6%	76.4%
Share of total before-tax income	100.0	4.6	8.4	9.0	82.7
Share of total spending	100.0	4.2	8.9	9.9	81.3
Travel	100.0	5.6	4.0	7.0	89.1
Airline fares	100.0	10.2	4.3	7.5	88.2
Alcoholic beverages purchased on trips	100.0	2.7	2.8	7.2	90.0
Bus fares, intercity	100.0	8.0	7.1	10.1	83.2
Gasoline on trips	100.0	3.0	4.5	8.1	87.5
Groceries on trips	100.0	3.8	3.5	8.5	88.1
Lodging on trips	100.0	3.5	4.0	5.0	91.1
Luggage	100.0	10.8	2.1	3.9	93.4
Parking fees and tolls on trips	100.0	4.6	4.8	7.4	88.1
Recreational expenses on trips	100.0	4.9	2.9	8.9	88.1
Restaurants and carry-outs on trips	100.0	4.6	3.9	7.2	89.0
Ship fares	100.0	5.6	2.7	3.1	94.3
Taxis and local transportation on trips	100.0	5.0	4.0	10.5	85.7
Train fares, intercity	100.0	4.7	3.8	6.4	89.7
Vehicle rental on trips	100.0	4.9	5.5	6.0	88.6

Note: "Asian" and "black" include Hispanics and non-Hispanics who identify themselves as being of the respective race alone. "Hispanic" includes people of any race who identify themselves as Hispanic. "Other" includes people who identify themselves as non-Hispanic and as Alaska Native, American Indian, Asian (who are also included in the Asian column), Native Hawaiian or other Pacific Islander, as well as non-Hispanics reporting more than one race.
Source: Calculations by New Strategist based on the Bureau of Labor Statistics' 2008 Consumer Expenditure Survey

Table 24. Travel: Average spending by region, 2008

(average annual spending of consumer units on travel, by region in which consumer unit lives, 2008)

	total consumer units	Northeast	Midwest	South	West
Number of consumer units (in 000s)	120,770	22,348	27,786	43,696	26,941
Number of persons per consumer unit	2.5	2.4	2.4	2.5	2.6
Average before-tax income of consumer units	$63,563.00	$70,436.00	$61,063.00	$58,881.00	$68,031.00
Average spending of consumer units, total	50,485.67	54,917.77	47,845.93	46,823.46	55,452.85
Travel	**1,417.96**	**1,560.40**	**1,332.95**	**1,112.14**	**1,883.44**
Airline fares	343.30	419.37	281.17	232.54	523.93
Alcoholic beverages purchased on trips	40.05	46.84	40.03	30.11	50.57
Bus fares, intercity	11.07	15.50	9.52	8.37	13.38
Gasoline on trips	144.54	105.37	170.16	129.60	174.86
Groceries on trips	48.80	53.91	45.20	39.04	64.12
Lodging on trips	328.71	382.90	318.66	269.43	390.28
Luggage	12.44	19.52	6.22	10.26	16.40
Parking fees and tolls on trips	10.35	16.70	9.21	8.55	9.18
Recreational expenses on trips	134.38	133.44	128.25	110.03	180.98
Restaurants and carry-outs on trips	237.87	250.49	223.35	199.16	305.15
Ship fares	37.83	38.63	37.28	25.99	56.92
Taxis and local transportation on trips	19.54	23.92	15.02	15.35	27.35
Train fares, intercity	22.36	27.88	23.26	15.68	27.70
Vehicle rental on trips	26.72	25.93	25.62	18.03	42.62

Source: Bureau of Labor Statistics, unpublished data from the 2008 Consumer Expenditure Survey; calculations by New Strategist

Table 25. Travel: Indexed spending by region, 2008

(indexed average annual spending of consumer units on travel by region in which consumer unit lives, 2008; index definition: an index of 100 is the average for all consumer units; an index of 132 means that spending by consumer units in that group is 32 percent above the average for all consumer units; an index of 68 indicates spending that is 32 percent below the average for all consumer units)

	total consumer units	Northeast	Midwest	South	West
Average spending of consumer units, total	**$50,486**	**$54,918**	**$47,846**	**$46,823**	**$55,453**
Average spending of consumer units, index	**100**	**109**	**95**	**93**	**110**
Travel	**100**	**110**	**94**	**78**	**133**
Airline fares	100	122	82	68	153
Alcoholic beverages purchased on trips	100	117	100	75	126
Bus fares, intercity	100	140	86	76	121
Gasoline on trips	100	73	118	90	121
Groceries on trips	100	110	93	80	131
Lodging on trips	100	116	97	82	119
Luggage	100	157	50	82	132
Parking fees and tolls on trips	100	161	89	83	89
Recreational expenses on trips	100	99	95	82	135
Restaurants and carry-outs on trips	100	105	94	84	128
Ship fares	100	102	99	69	150
Taxis and local transportation on trips	100	122	77	79	140
Train fares, intercity	100	125	104	70	124
Vehicle rental on trips	100	97	96	67	160

Source: Calculations by New Strategist based on the Bureau of Labor Statistics' 2008 Consumer Expenditure Survey

Table 26. Travel: Total spending by region, 2008

(total annual spending on travel, by region in which consumer unit lives, 2008; consumer units and dollars in thousands)

	total consumer units	Northeast	Midwest	South	West
Number of consumer units	120,770	22,348	27,786	43,696	26,941
Total spending of all consumer units	$6,097,154,366	$1,227,302,324	$1,329,447,011	$2,045,997,908	$1,493,955,232
Travel	**171,247,029**	**34,871,819**	**37,037,349**	**48,596,069**	**50,741,757**
Airline fares	41,460,341	9,372,081	7,812,590	10,161,068	14,115,198
Alcoholic beverages purchased on trips	4,836,839	1,046,780	1,112,274	1,315,687	1,362,406
Bus fares, intercity	1,336,924	346,394	264,523	365,736	360,471
Gasoline on trips	17,456,096	2,354,809	4,728,066	5,663,002	4,710,903
Groceries on trips	5,893,576	1,204,781	1,255,927	1,705,892	1,727,457
Lodging on trips	39,698,307	8,557,049	8,854,287	11,773,013	10,514,533
Luggage	1,502,379	436,233	172,829	448,321	441,832
Parking fees and tolls on trips	1,249,970	373,212	255,909	373,601	247,318
Recreational expenses on trips	16,229,073	2,982,117	3,563,555	4,807,871	4,875,782
Restaurants and carry-outs on trips	28,727,560	5,597,951	6,206,003	8,702,495	8,221,046
Ship fares	4,568,729	863,303	1,035,862	1,135,659	1,533,482
Taxis and local transportation on trips	2,359,846	534,564	417,346	670,734	736,836
Train fares, intercity	2,700,417	623,062	646,302	685,153	746,266
Vehicle rental on trips	3,226,974	579,484	711,877	787,839	1,148,225

Note: Numbers may not add to total because of rounding.
Source: Calculations by New Strategist based on the Bureau of Labor Statistics' 2008 Consumer Expenditure Survey

Table 27. Travel: Market shares by region, 2008

(percentage of total annual spending on travel accounted for by consumer units by region of residence, 2008)

	total consumer units	Northeast	Midwest	South	West
Share of total consumer units	100.0%	18.5%	23.0%	36.2%	22.3%
Share of total before-tax income	100.0	20.5	22.1	33.5	23.9
Share of total spending	100.0	20.1	21.8	33.6	24.5
Travel	100.0	20.4	21.6	28.4	29.6
Airline fares	100.0	22.6	18.8	24.5	34.0
Alcoholic beverages purchased on trips	100.0	21.6	23.0	27.2	28.2
Bus fares, intercity	100.0	25.9	19.8	27.4	27.0
Gasoline on trips	100.0	13.5	27.1	32.4	27.0
Groceries on trips	100.0	20.4	21.3	28.9	29.3
Lodging on trips	100.0	21.6	22.3	29.7	26.5
Luggage	100.0	29.0	11.5	29.8	29.4
Parking fees and tolls on trips	100.0	29.9	20.5	29.9	19.8
Recreational expenses on trips	100.0	18.4	22.0	29.6	30.0
Restaurants and carry-outs on trips	100.0	19.5	21.6	30.3	28.6
Ship fares	100.0	18.9	22.7	24.9	33.6
Taxis and local transportation on trips	100.0	22.7	17.7	28.4	31.2
Train fares, intercity	100.0	23.1	23.9	25.4	27.6
Vehicle rental on trips	100.0	18.0	22.1	24.4	35.6

Note: Numbers may not add to total because of rounding.
Source: Calculations by New Strategist based on the Bureau of Labor Statistics' 2008 Consumer Expenditure Survey

Table 28. Travel: Average spending by education, 2008

(average annual spending of consumer units (CU) on travel, by education of consumer unit reference person, 2008)

	total consumer units	less than high school graduate	high school graduate	some college	associate's degree	college graduate total	bachelor's degree	master's, professional, doctorate
Number of consumer units (in 000s)	120,770	17,600	30,761	26,386	11,097	34,925	22,428	12,498
Number of persons per CU	2.5	2.6	2.5	2.4	2.5	2.5	2.5	2.4
Average before-tax income of CU	$63,563.00	$32,909.00	$48,364.00	$55,403.00	$63,964.00	$98,434.00	$88,888.00	$115,564.00
Average spending of CU, total	50,485.67	29,903.26	40,849.92	47,204.79	53,385.33	70,857.87	66,221.12	79,198.33
Travel	**1,417.96**	**351.81**	**764.64**	**1,150.27**	**1,349.98**	**2,754.45**	**2,224.25**	**3,706.50**
Airline fares	343.30	81.29	145.57	242.49	281.37	745.34	572.49	1,055.52
Alcoholic beverages purchased on trips	40.05	8.03	19.04	35.25	37.73	79.07	66.37	101.85
Bus fares, intercity	11.07	4.15	7.50	11.06	9.84	18.11	14.37	24.81
Gasoline on trips	144.54	58.85	108.28	144.09	162.22	214.40	195.69	247.99
Groceries on trips	48.80	15.70	30.99	47.40	47.21	82.73	72.23	101.59
Lodging on trips	328.71	74.24	180.43	256.47	305.47	649.52	538.66	848.46
Luggage	12.44	2.61	8.04	11.04	19.66	19.94	11.59	35.49
Parking fees and tolls on trips	10.35	3.04	5.67	8.68	9.05	19.84	15.55	27.53
Recreational expenses on trips	134.38	24.77	73.63	120.86	127.23	255.60	201.36	352.95
Restaurants and carry-outs on trips	237.87	60.95	128.08	203.65	241.11	448.54	360.17	607.13
Ship fares	37.83	7.46	21.68	25.41	40.62	75.84	68.99	88.12
Taxis and local transportation on trips	19.54	3.28	8.99	12.26	25.83	40.52	29.46	60.38
Train fares, intercity	22.36	2.97	12.76	16.21	17.58	46.75	34.60	68.55
Vehicle rental on trips	26.72	4.47	13.98	15.40	25.06	58.25	42.72	86.13

Source: Bureau of Labor Statistics, unpublished data from the 2008 Consumer Expenditure Survey; calculations by New Strategist

Table 29. Travel: Indexed spending by education, 2008

(indexed average annual spending of consumer units (CU) on travel by education of consumer unit reference person, 2008; index definition: an index of 100 is the average for all consumer units; an index of 132 means that spending by consumer units in that group is 32 percent above the average for all consumer units; an index of 68 indicates spending that is 32 percent below the average for all consumer units)

	total consumer units	less than high school graduate	high school graduate	some college	associate's degree	college graduate total	bachelor's degree	master's, professional, doctorate
Average spending of CU, total	$50,486	$29,903	$40,850	$47,205	$53,385	$70,858	$66,221	$79,198
Average spending of CU, index	100	59	81	94	106	140	131	157
Travel	**100**	**25**	**54**	**81**	**95**	**194**	**157**	**261**
Airline fares	100	24	42	71	82	217	167	307
Alcoholic beverages purchased on trips	100	20	48	88	94	197	166	254
Bus fares, intercity	100	37	68	100	89	164	130	224
Gasoline on trips	100	41	75	100	112	148	135	172
Groceries on trips	100	32	64	97	97	170	148	208
Lodging on trips	100	23	55	78	93	198	164	258
Luggage	100	21	65	89	158	160	93	285
Parking fees and tolls on trips	100	29	55	84	87	192	150	266
Recreational expenses on trips	100	18	55	90	95	190	150	263
Restaurants and carry-outs on trips	100	26	54	86	101	189	151	255
Ship fares	100	20	57	67	107	200	182	233
Taxis and local transportation on trips	100	17	46	63	132	207	151	309
Train fares, intercity	100	13	57	72	79	209	155	307
Vehicle rental on trips	100	17	52	58	94	218	160	322

Source: Calculations by New Strategist based on the Bureau of Labor Statistics' 2008 Consumer Expenditure Survey

Table 30. Travel: Total spending by education, 2008

(total annual spending on travel, by consumer unit (CU) educational attainment group, 2008; consumer units and dollars in thousands)

	total consumer units	less than high school graduate	high school graduate	some college	associate's degree	college graduate total	bachelor's degree	master's, professional, doctorate
Number of consumer units	120,770	17,600	30,761	26,386	11,097	34,925	22,428	12,498
Total spending of all CUs	$6,097,154,366	$526,297,376	$1,256,584,389	$1,245,545,589	$592,417,007	$2,474,711,110	$1,485,207,279	$989,820,728
Travel	**171,247,029**	**6,191,856**	**23,521,091**	**30,351,024**	**14,980,728**	**96,199,166**	**49,885,479**	**46,323,837**
Airline fares	41,460,341	1,430,704	4,477,879	6,398,341	3,122,363	26,031,000	12,839,806	13,191,889
Alcoholic beverages purchased on trips	4,836,839	141,328	585,689	930,107	418,690	2,761,520	1,488,546	1,272,921
Bus fares, intercity	1,336,924	73,040	230,708	291,829	109,194	632,492	322,290	310,075
Gasoline on trips	17,456,096	1,035,760	3,330,801	3,801,959	1,800,155	7,487,920	4,388,935	3,099,379
Groceries on trips	5,893,576	276,320	953,283	1,250,696	523,889	2,889,345	1,619,974	1,269,672
Lodging on trips	39,698,307	1,306,624	5,550,207	6,767,217	3,389,801	22,684,486	12,081,066	10,604,053
Luggage	1,502,379	45,936	247,318	291,301	218,167	696,405	259,941	443,554
Parking fees and tolls on trips	1,249,970	53,504	174,415	229,030	100,428	692,912	348,755	344,070
Recreational expenses on trips	16,229,073	435,952	2,264,932	3,189,012	1,411,871	8,926,830	4,516,102	4,411,169
Restaurants and carry-outs on trips	28,727,560	1,072,720	3,939,869	5,373,509	2,675,598	15,665,260	8,077,893	7,587,911
Ship fares	4,568,729	131,296	666,898	670,468	450,760	2,648,712	1,547,308	1,101,324
Taxis and local transportation on trips	2,359,846	57,728	276,541	323,492	286,636	1,415,161	660,729	754,629
Train fares, intercity	2,700,417	52,272	392,510	427,717	195,085	1,632,744	776,009	856,738
Vehicle rental on trips	3,226,974	78,672	430,039	406,344	278,091	2,034,381	958,124	1,076,453

Note: Numbers may not add to total because of rounding.
Source: Calculations by New Strategist based on the Bureau of Labor Statistics' 2008 Consumer Expenditure Survey

Table 31. Travel: Market shares by education, 2008

(percentage of total annual spending on travel accounted for by consumer unit educational attainment groups, 2008)

	total consumer units	less than high school graduate	high school graduate	some college	associate's degree	college graduate total	bachelor's degree	master's, professional, doctorate
Share of total consumer units	100.0%	14.6%	25.5%	21.8%	9.2%	28.9%	18.6%	10.3%
Share of total before-tax income	100.0	7.5	19.4	19.0	9.2	44.8	26.0	18.8
Share of total spending	100.0	8.6	20.6	20.4	9.7	40.6	24.4	16.2
Travel	**100.0**	**3.6**	**13.7**	**17.7**	**8.7**	**56.2**	**29.1**	**27.1**
Airline fares	100.0	3.5	10.8	15.4	7.5	62.8	31.0	31.8
Alcoholic beverages purchased on trips	100.0	2.9	12.1	19.2	8.7	57.1	30.8	26.3
Bus fares, intercity	100.0	5.5	17.3	21.8	8.2	47.3	24.1	23.2
Gasoline on trips	100.0	5.9	19.1	21.8	10.3	42.9	25.1	17.8
Groceries on trips	100.0	4.7	16.2	21.2	8.9	49.0	27.5	21.5
Lodging on trips	100.0	3.3	14.0	17.0	8.5	57.1	30.4	26.7
Luggage	100.0	3.1	16.5	19.4	14.5	46.4	17.3	29.5
Parking fees and tolls on trips	100.0	4.3	14.0	18.3	8.0	55.4	27.9	27.5
Recreational expenses on trips	100.0	2.7	14.0	19.6	8.7	55.0	27.8	27.2
Restaurants and carry-outs on trips	100.0	3.7	13.7	18.7	9.3	54.5	28.1	26.4
Ship fares	100.0	2.9	14.6	14.7	9.9	58.0	33.9	24.1
Taxis and local transportation on trips	100.0	2.4	11.7	13.7	12.1	60.0	28.0	32.0
Train fares, intercity	100.0	1.9	14.5	15.8	7.2	60.5	28.7	31.7
Vehicle rental on trips	100.0	2.4	13.3	12.6	8.6	63.0	29.7	33.4

Note: Numbers may not add to total because of rounding.
Source: Calculations by New Strategist based on the Bureau of Labor Statistics' 2008 Consumer Expenditure Survey

Airline Fares

Best customers:	**Householders aged 45 to 64**
	Married couples without children at home
	Married couples with school-aged or older children at home
	Asians
	Households in the Northeast and West
	College graduates
Customer trends:	**Average household spending on airline fares is likely to decline because**
	of the economic downturn, despite the presence of baby boomers in the
	peak-spending age groups.

The biggest spenders on airline fares are college-educated, middle-aged adults. Householders aged 45 to 64 spend 28 to 31 percent more than average on airfares and account for 49 percent of the market. College graduates spend over twice the average on airfares and account for 63 percent of the market. Married couples without children at home (most of them empty-nesters) spend 48 percent more than average on airfares, while those with school-aged or older children spend 45 to 58 percent more than average on this item. Asians spend more than two-and-one-half times the average on airfares. Households in the West spend 53 percent more than average on airline fares, and those in the Northeast spend 22 percent more.

Average household spending on airline fares held steady between 2000 and 2008, after adjusting for inflation. Average household spending on airline fares is likely to decline because of the economic downturn, despite the presence of baby boomers in the peak-spending age groups.

Table 32. Airline fares

Total household spending	$41,460,341,000.00
Average household spends	343.30

	AVERAGE HOUSEHOLD SPENDING	BEST CUSTOMERS (index)	BIGGEST CUSTOMERS (market share)
AGE OF HOUSEHOLDER			
Average household	**$343.30**	**100**	**100.0%**
Under age 25	117.87	34	2.3
Aged 25 to 34	258.50	75	12.6
Aged 35 to 44	379.87	111	20.9
Aged 45 to 54	440.12	128	27.2
Aged 55 to 64	449.52	131	21.5
Aged 65 to 74	323.83	94	9.8
Aged 75 or older	203.29	59	5.6

	AVERAGE HOUSEHOLD SPENDING	BEST CUSTOMERS (index)	BIGGEST CUSTOMERS (market share)
HOUSEHOLD INCOME			
Average household	**$343.30**	**100**	**100.0%**
Under $20,000	99.45	29	6.1
$20,000 to $39,999	138.81	40	9.0
$40,000 to $49,999	161.86	47	4.4
$50,000 to $69,999	270.85	79	11.9
$70,000 to $79,999	345.34	101	6.1
$80,000 to $99,999	420.63	123	10.2
$100,000 or more	1,002.84	292	52.3
HOUSEHOLD TYPE			
Average household	**343.30**	**100**	**100.0**
Married couples	487.22	142	72.0
Married couples, no children	509.37	148	33.1
Married couples, with children	476.79	139	34.3
Oldest child under age 6	307.46	90	4.0
Oldest child aged 6 to 17	497.85	145	18.6
Oldest child aged 18 or older	541.21	158	11.7
Single parent with child under age 18	175.82	51	3.0
Single person	188.73	55	16.0
RACE AND HISPANIC ORIGIN			
Average household	**343.30**	**100**	**100.0**
Asian	921.35	268	10.2
Black	120.15	35	4.3
Hispanic	223.89	65	7.5
Non-Hispanic white and other	396.44	115	88.2
REGION			
Average household	**343.30**	**100**	**100.0**
Northeast	419.37	122	22.6
Midwest	281.17	82	18.8
South	232.54	68	24.5
West	523.93	153	34.0
EDUCATION			
Average household	**343.30**	**100**	**100.0**
Less than high school graduate	81.29	24	3.5
High school graduate	145.57	42	10.8
Some college	242.49	71	15.4
Associate's degree	281.37	82	7.5
College graduate	745.34	217	62.8
Bachelor's degree	572.49	167	31.0
Master's, professional, doctoral degree	1,055.52	307	31.8

t

Note: Market shares may not sum to 100.0 because of rounding and missing categories by household type. "Asian" and "black" include Hispanics and non-Hispanics who identify themselves as being of the respective race alone. "Hispanic" includes people of any race who identify themselves as Hispanic. "Other" includes people who identify themselves as non-Hispanic and as Alaska Native, American Indian, Asian (who are also included in the Asian row), Native Hawaiian or other Pacific Islander, as well as non-Hispanics reporting more than one race.
Source: Calculations by New Strategist based on the Bureau of Labor Statistics' 2008 Consumer Expenditure Survey

Alcoholic Beverages Purchased on Trips

Best customers: Householders aged 45 to 64
Married couples without children at home
Non-Hispanic whites

Customer trends: Average household spending on alcoholic beverages while traveling
should continue to grow as more boomers become empty-nesters, but
only if discretionary income grows.

The biggest spenders on alcoholic beverages purchased on trips are older, white, married travelers. Householders aged 45 to 64 spend 17 to 30 percent more than average on this item and account for 46 percent of the market. Married couples without children at home (most of them older) spend 59 percent more than average on alcoholic beverages while on trips. These empty-nesters spend more than other household types on alcoholic beverages while traveling because they no longer need to devote their time and money to children's wants and needs. Non-Hispanic whites spend 18 percent more than average on alcoholic beverages while traveling, while all the other racial and ethnic groups spend considerably less than average.

Average household spending on alcoholic beverages purchased on trips fell 6 percent between 2000 and 2008, after adjusting for inflation. Behind the decline was the economic downturn, which reduced spending on travel. In the years ahead, spending on this item should grow as more boomers become empty-nesters, but only if discretionary income grows.

Table 33. Alcoholic beverages purchased on trips

Total household spending $4,836,838,500.00
Average household spends   40.05

	AVERAGE HOUSEHOLD SPENDING	BEST CUSTOMERS (index)	BIGGEST CUSTOMERS (market share)
AGE OF HOUSEHOLDER			
Average household	**$40.05**	**100**	**100.0%**
Under age 25	21.42	53	3.6
Aged 25 to 34	38.89	97	16.2
Aged 35 to 44	39.08	98	18.4
Aged 45 to 54	46.83	117	24.8
Aged 55 to 64	52.06	130	21.3
Aged 65 to 74	37.23	93	9.7
Aged 75 or older	24.62	61	5.8

	AVERAGE HOUSEHOLD SPENDING	BEST CUSTOMERS (index)	BIGGEST CUSTOMERS (market share)
HOUSEHOLD INCOME			
Average household	**$40.05**	**100**	**100.0%**
Under $20,000	10.94	27	5.7
$20,000 to $39,999	16.95	42	9.4
$40,000 to $49,999	26.45	66	6.2
$50,000 to $69,999	29.14	73	11.0
$70,000 to $79,999	34.02	85	5.2
$80,000 to $99,999	50.85	127	10.5
$100,000 or more	116.29	290	52.0
HOUSEHOLD TYPE			
Average household	**40.05**	**100**	**100.0**
Married couples	50.80	127	64.3
Married couples, no children	63.68	159	35.4
Married couples, with children	42.40	106	26.1
Oldest child under age 6	37.39	93	4.1
Oldest child aged 6 to 17	42.87	107	13.7
Oldest child aged 18 or older	44.57	111	8.3
Single parent with child under age 18	18.59	46	2.7
Single person	29.62	74	21.5
RACE AND HISPANIC ORIGIN			
Average household	**40.05**	**100**	**100.0**
Asian	27.83	69	2.7
Black	9.22	23	2.8
Hispanic	24.99	62	7.2
Non-Hispanic white and other	47.21	118	90.0
REGION			
Average household	**40.05**	**100**	**100.0**
Northeast	46.84	117	21.6
Midwest	40.03	100	23.0
South	30.11	75	27.2
West	50.57	126	28.2
EDUCATION			
Average household	**40.05**	**100**	**100.0**
Less than high school graduate	8.03	20	2.9
High school graduate	19.04	48	12.1
Some college	35.25	88	19.2
Associate's degree	37.73	94	8.7
College graduate	79.07	197	57.1
Bachelor's degree	66.37	166	30.8
Master's, professional, doctoral degree	101.85	254	26.3

Note: Market shares may not sum to 100.0 because of rounding and missing categories by household type. "Asian" and "black" include Hispanics and non-Hispanics who identify themselves as being of the respective race alone. "Hispanic" includes people of any race who identify themselves as Hispanic. "Other" includes people who identify themselves as non-Hispanic and as Alaska Native, American Indian, Asian (who are also included in the Asian row), Native Hawaiian or other Pacific Islander, as well as non-Hispanics reporting more than one race.
Source: Calculations by New Strategist based on the Bureau of Labor Statistics' 2008 Consumer Expenditure Survey

Bus Fares, Intercity

Best customers: **Householders aged 65 to 74**
                             Married couples without children at home
                             Asians
                             Households in the Northeast and West

Customer trends: **Average household spending on intercity bus fares may stabilize as**
                             boomers fill the best-customer age group and the economic downturn reduces
                             discretionary income.

The best customers of intercity bus fares are older travelers. Householders aged 65 to 74 spend 47 percent more than average on this item. Married couples without children at home, most of them empty-nesters, spend 77 percent more than average on intercity bus fares and account for 39 percent of the market. Asians spend more than twice the average amount on intercity bus travel. Households in the Northeast and West spend, respectively, 40 and 21 percent more than average on bus fares.

Average household spending on intercity bus fares fell by a substantial 45 percent between 2000 and 2008, after adjusting for inflation. Average household spending on intercity bus fares may stabilize as boomers fill the best-customer age group and the economic downturn reduces discretionary income.

Table 34. Bus fares, intercity

Total household spending	$1,336,923,900.00
Average household spends	11.07

	AVERAGE HOUSEHOLD SPENDING	BEST CUSTOMERS (index)	BIGGEST CUSTOMERS (market share)
AGE OF HOUSEHOLDER			
Average household	**$11.07**	**100**	**100.0%**
Under age 25	6.27	57	3.9
Aged 25 to 34	8.54	77	12.9
Aged 35 to 44	9.29	84	15.9
Aged 45 to 54	11.81	107	22.6
Aged 55 to 64	12.70	115	18.8
Aged 65 to 74	16.31	147	15.3
Aged 75 or older	12.33	111	10.6

	AVERAGE HOUSEHOLD SPENDING	BEST CUSTOMERS (index)	BIGGEST CUSTOMERS (market share)
HOUSEHOLD INCOME			
Average household	**$11.07**	**100**	**100.0%**
Under $20,000	5.86	53	11.1
$20,000 to $39,999	8.28	75	16.7
$40,000 to $49,999	7.21	65	6.1
$50,000 to $69,999	8.34	75	11.4
$70,000 to $79,999	8.51	77	4.7
$80,000 to $99,999	11.56	104	8.7
$100,000 or more	25.64	232	41.5
HOUSEHOLD TYPE			
Average household	**11.07**	**100**	**100.0**
Married couples	13.74	124	62.9
Married couples, no children	19.56	177	39.4
Married couples, with children	9.46	85	21.1
Oldest child under age 6	4.84	44	1.9
Oldest child aged 6 to 17	10.38	94	12.0
Oldest child aged 18 or older	10.63	96	7.1
Single parent with child under age 18	5.85	53	3.1
Single person	9.56	86	25.1
RACE AND HISPANIC ORIGIN			
Average household	**11.07**	**100**	**100.0**
Asian	23.08	208	8.0
Black	6.42	58	7.1
Hispanic	9.64	87	10.1
Non-Hispanic white and other	12.06	109	83.2
REGION			
Average household	**11.07**	**100**	**100.0**
Northeast	15.50	140	25.9
Midwest	9.52	86	19.8
South	8.37	76	27.4
West	13.38	121	27.0
EDUCATION			
Average household	**11.07**	**100**	**100.0**
Less than high school graduate	4.15	37	5.5
High school graduate	7.50	68	17.3
Some college	11.06	100	21.8
Associate's degree	9.84	89	8.2
College graduate	18.11	164	47.3
Bachelor's degree	14.37	130	24.1
Master's, professional, doctoral degree	24.81	224	23.2

Note: Market shares may not sum to 100.0 because of rounding and missing categories by household type. "Asian" and "black" include Hispanics and non-Hispanics who identify themselves as being of the respective race alone. "Hispanic" includes people of any race who identify themselves as Hispanic. "Other" includes people who identify themselves as non-Hispanic and as Alaska Native, American Indian, Asian (who are also included in the Asian row), Native Hawaiian or other Pacific Islander, as well as non-Hispanics reporting more than one race.
Source: Calculations by New Strategist based on the Bureau of Labor Statistics' 2008 Consumer Expenditure Survey

Gasoline on Trips

Best customers: Householders aged 35 to 74

Married couples without children at home

Married couples with school-aged or older children at home

Customer trends: Average household spending on gasoline while traveling should continue to rise

in the next few years as more boomers fill the peak-traveling lifestage.

The biggest spenders on gasoline purchased while traveling are the largest households as well as the most avid travelers—empty-nesters. Householders aged 55 to 64 spend 25 percent more than average on this item and account for one-fifth of the market. Married couples without children at home (most of them empty-nesters) spend 49 percent more than average on gasoline while traveling and account for one-third of the market. Couples with school-aged or older children at home spend 29 to 54 more than average on this item.

Average household spending on gasoline while on trips rose 26 percent between 2000 and 2008, after adjusting for inflation, as gas prices increased. Average household spending on gasoline while traveling should continue to rise in the next few years as more boomers fill the peak-traveling lifestage.

Table 35. Gasoline on trips

Total household spending $17,456,095,800.00
Average household spends   144.54

	AVERAGE HOUSEHOLD SPENDING	BEST CUSTOMERS (index)	BIGGEST CUSTOMERS (market share)
AGE OF HOUSEHOLDER			
Average household	**$144.54**	**100**	**100.0%**
Under age 25	77.74	54	3.7
Aged 25 to 34	137.22	95	15.9
Aged 35 to 44	154.87	107	20.3
Aged 45 to 54	161.59	112	23.7
Aged 55 to 64	181.14	125	20.6
Aged 65 to 74	156.24	108	11.3
Aged 75 or older	70.71	49	4.7

	AVERAGE HOUSEHOLD SPENDING	BEST CUSTOMERS (index)	BIGGEST CUSTOMERS (market share)
HOUSEHOLD INCOME			
Average household	**$144.54**	**100**	**100.0%**
Under $20,000	53.07	37	7.7
$20,000 to $39,999	95.20	66	14.7
$40,000 to $49,999	116.72	81	7.5
$50,000 to $69,999	150.68	104	15.8
$70,000 to $79,999	205.40	142	8.7
$80,000 to $99,999	218.62	151	12.5
$100,000 or more	267.37	185	33.1
HOUSEHOLD TYPE			
Average household	**144.54**	**100**	**100.0**
Married couples	203.93	141	71.5
Married couples, no children	214.98	149	33.2
Married couples, with children	200.90	139	34.3
Oldest child under age 6	162.41	112	5.0
Oldest child aged 6 to 17	222.17	154	19.7
Oldest child aged 18 or older	187.13	129	9.6
Single parent with child under age 18	84.41	58	3.4
Single person	76.95	53	15.5
RACE AND HISPANIC ORIGIN			
Average household	**144.54**	**100**	**100.0**
Asian	111.90	77	3.0
Black	53.11	37	4.5
Hispanic	101.24	70	8.1
Non-Hispanic white and other	165.59	115	87.5
REGION			
Average household	**144.54**	**100**	**100.0**
Northeast	105.37	73	13.5
Midwest	170.16	118	27.1
South	129.60	90	32.4
West	174.86	121	27.0
EDUCATION			
Average household	**144.54**	**100**	**100.0**
Less than high school graduate	58.85	41	5.9
High school graduate	108.28	75	19.1
Some college	144.09	100	21.8
Associate's degree	162.22	112	10.3
College graduate	214.40	148	42.9
Bachelor's degree	195.69	135	25.1
Master's, professional, doctoral degree	247.99	172	17.8

Note: Market shares may not sum to 100.0 because of rounding and missing categories by household type. "Asian" and "black" include Hispanics and non-Hispanics who identify themselves as being of the respective race alone. "Hispanic" includes people of any race who identify themselves as Hispanic. "Other" includes people who identify themselves as non-Hispanic and as Alaska Native, American Indian, Asian (who are also included in the Asian row), Native Hawaiian or other Pacific Islander, as well as non-Hispanics reporting more than one race.
Source: Calculations by New Strategist based on the Bureau of Labor Statistics' 2008 Consumer Expenditure Survey

Groceries on Trips

Best customers: Householders aged 55 to 64
Married couples without children at home
Married couples with school-aged or older children at home
Households in the West

Customer trends: Average household spending on groceries while traveling should rise in the next few years as more boomers become empty-nesters.

The biggest spenders on groceries purchased on trips are older married couples, the most avid travelers. These couples are stocking up on food and drink for their hotel rooms or RVs. Householders aged 55 to 64 spend 51 percent more than average on this item. Married couples without children at home (most of them empty-nesters) spend 55 percent more than average on groceries while traveling and account for over one-third of the market. Couples with school-aged or older children at home spend 43 to 47 percent more than average. Households in the West spend 31 percent more than average on this item.

Average household spending on groceries while traveling fell 2 percent between 2000 and 2008, after adjusting for inflation. Behind the decline was the economic downturn, which reduced spending on travel. Average household spending on groceries while traveling should rise in the next few years as more boomers become empty-nesters.

Table 36. Groceries on trips

Total household spending $5,893,576,000.00
Average household spends   48.80

	AVERAGE HOUSEHOLD SPENDING	BEST CUSTOMERS (index)	BIGGEST CUSTOMERS (market share)
AGE OF HOUSEHOLDER			
Average household	**$48.80**	**100**	**100.0%**
Under age 25	14.97	31	2.1
Aged 25 to 34	33.78	69	11.6
Aged 35 to 44	51.12	105	19.8
Aged 45 to 54	57.30	117	24.9
Aged 55 to 64	73.66	151	24.8
Aged 65 to 74	56.77	116	12.1
Aged 75 or older	24.26	50	4.7

	AVERAGE HOUSEHOLD SPENDING	BEST CUSTOMERS (index)	BIGGEST CUSTOMERS (market share)
HOUSEHOLD INCOME			
Average household	**$48.80**	**100**	**100.0%**
Under $20,000	16.59	34	7.1
$20,000 to $39,999	28.65	59	13.1
$40,000 to $49,999	34.82	71	6.7
$50,000 to $69,999	44.93	92	13.9
$70,000 to $79,999	55.22	113	6.9
$80,000 to $99,999	74.46	153	12.7
$100,000 or more	108.10	222	39.6
HOUSEHOLD TYPE			
Average household	**48.80**	**100**	**100.0**
Married couples	69.55	143	72.3
Married couples, no children	75.86	155	34.6
Married couples, with children	67.32	138	34.0
Oldest child under age 6	50.36	103	4.6
Oldest child aged 6 to 17	71.89	147	18.9
Oldest child aged 18 or older	69.54	143	10.6
Single parent with child under age 18	26.68	55	3.2
Single person	24.76	51	14.7
RACE AND HISPANIC ORIGIN			
Average household	**48.80**	**100**	**100.0**
Asian	48.81	100	3.8
Black	13.91	29	3.5
Hispanic	35.88	74	8.5
Non-Hispanic white and other	56.32	115	88.1
REGION			
Average household	**48.80**	**100**	**100.0**
Northeast	53.91	110	20.4
Midwest	45.20	93	21.3
South	39.04	80	28.9
West	64.12	131	29.3
EDUCATION			
Average household	**48.80**	**100**	**100.0**
Less than high school graduate	15.70	32	4.7
High school graduate	30.99	64	16.2
Some college	47.40	97	21.2
Associate's degree	47.21	97	8.9
College graduate	82.73	170	49.0
Bachelor's degree	72.23	148	27.5
Master's, professional, doctoral degree	101.59	208	21.5

Note: Market shares may not sum to 100.0 because of rounding and missing categories by household type. "Asian" and "black" include Hispanics and non-Hispanics who identify themselves as being of the respective race alone. "Hispanic" includes people of any race who identify themselves as Hispanic. "Other" includes people who identify themselves as non-Hispanic and as Alaska Native, American Indian, Asian (who are also included in the Asian row), Native Hawaiian or other Pacific Islander, as well as non-Hispanics reporting more than one race.
Source: Calculations by New Strategist based on the Bureau of Labor Statistics' 2008 Consumer Expenditure Survey

Lodging on Trips

Best customers: Householders aged 45 to 64
                             Married couples without children at home
                             Married couples with school-aged or older children at home
                             Non-Hispanic whites

Customer trends: Average household spending on lodging should continue to grow as more
                             boomers become empty-nesters, but only if discretionary income rises.

Lodging is the second biggest travel expense after airline fares. It accounts for $23 of every $100 spent by the average household on travel. The biggest spenders on lodging are the most avid travelers—older empty-nesters. Householders aged 45 to 64 spend 33 to 41 percent more than average on this item and account for 51 percent of the market. Married couples without children at home (most of them empty-nesters) spend 63 percent more than average on lodging. Couples with school-aged or older children at home spend 54 to 59 percent more than the average household on lodging on trips and account for nearly one-third of the market. Non-Hispanic whites spend 19 percent more than average on lodging.

Average household spending on lodging rose 4 percent between 2000 and 2008, after adjusting for inflation. This rise in spending occurred as the baby-boom generation aged into the peak-spending lifestage. Average household spending on lodging should continue to grow as more boomers become empty-nesters, but only if discretionary income rises.

Table 37. Lodging on trips

Total household spending $39,698,306,700.00
Average household spends   328.71

	AVERAGE HOUSEHOLD SPENDING	BEST CUSTOMERS (index)	BIGGEST CUSTOMERS (market share)
AGE OF HOUSEHOLDER			
Average household	**$328.71**	**100**	**100.0%**
Under age 25	69.49	21	1.4
Aged 25 to 34	204.96	62	10.4
Aged 35 to 44	343.27	104	19.7
Aged 45 to 54	437.15	133	28.2
Aged 55 to 64	464.77	141	23.2
Aged 65 to 74	351.32	107	11.1
Aged 75 or older	201.66	61	5.8

	AVERAGE HOUSEHOLD SPENDING	BEST CUSTOMERS (index)	BIGGEST CUSTOMERS (market share)
HOUSEHOLD INCOME			
Average household	**$328.71**	**100**	**100.0%**
Under $20,000	76.90	23	4.9
$20,000 to $39,999	129.12	39	8.7
$40,000 to $49,999	187.49	57	5.3
$50,000 to $69,999	243.00	74	11.2
$70,000 to $79,999	315.90	96	5.9
$80,000 to $99,999	432.60	132	10.9
$100,000 or more	974.41	296	53.1
HOUSEHOLD TYPE			
Average household	**328.71**	**100**	**100.0**
Married couples	480.04	146	74.1
Married couples, no children	534.89	163	36.3
Married couples, with children	464.26	141	34.9
Oldest child under age 6	246.86	75	3.3
Oldest child aged 6 to 17	504.79	154	19.7
Oldest child aged 18 or older	523.73	159	11.8
Single parent with child under age 18	186.94	57	3.3
Single person	166.11	51	14.7
RACE AND HISPANIC ORIGIN			
Average household	**328.71**	**100**	**100.0**
Asian	301.06	92	3.5
Black	106.66	32	4.0
Hispanic	141.38	43	5.0
Non-Hispanic white and other	392.06	119	91.1
REGION			
Average household	**328.71**	**100**	**100.0**
Northeast	382.90	116	21.6
Midwest	318.66	97	22.3
South	269.43	82	29.7
West	390.28	119	26.5
EDUCATION			
Average household	**328.71**	**100**	**100.0**
Less than high school graduate	74.24	23	3.3
High school graduate	180.43	55	14.0
Some college	256.47	78	17.0
Associate's degree	305.47	93	8.5
College graduate	649.52	198	57.1
Bachelor's degree	538.66	164	30.4
Master's, professional, doctoral degree	848.46	258	26.7

Note: Market shares may not sum to 100.0 because of rounding and missing categories by household type. "Asian" and "black" include Hispanics and non-Hispanics who identify themselves as being of the respective race alone. "Hispanic" includes people of any race who identify themselves as Hispanic. "Other" includes people who identify themselves as non-Hispanic and as Alaska Native, American Indian, Asian (who are also included in the Asian row), Native Hawaiian or other Pacific Islander, as well as non-Hispanics reporting more than one race.
Source: Calculations by New Strategist based on the Bureau of Labor Statistics' 2008 Consumer Expenditure Survey

Luggage

Best customers:

Householders aged 45 to 54
Married couples with adult children at home
Asians and non-Hispanic whites
Households in the Northeast and West

Customer trends:

Average household spending on luggage could continue to grow as more boomers become empty-nesters, but the economic downturn and the loss of discretionary income may hurt this market.

The biggest spenders on luggage are middle-aged married couples with adult children at home. Householders aged 45 to 54 spend more than twice the average on this item and control 43 percent of the market. Married couples with adult children at home spend over three times the average on this item. Asians, a relatively affluent group, spend close to three times the average on luggage. Non-Hispanic whites spend 22 percent more. Households in the Northeast and West spend, respectively, 57 and 32 percent above average on luggage.

Average household spending on luggage rose 20 percent between 2000 and 2008, after adjusting for inflation. Average household spending on luggage could continue to grow as more boomers become empty-nesters, but the economic downturn and the loss of discretionary income may hurt this market.

Table 38. Luggage

Total household spending $1,502,378,800.00
Average household spends 12.44

	AVERAGE HOUSEHOLD SPENDING	BEST CUSTOMERS (index)	BIGGEST CUSTOMERS (market share)
AGE OF HOUSEHOLDER			
Average household	**$12.44**	**100**	**100.0%**
Under age 25	3.51	28	1.9
Aged 25 to 34	11.08	89	14.9
Aged 35 to 44	13.42	108	20.4
Aged 45 to 54	25.34	204	43.2
Aged 55 to 64	10.01	80	13.2
Aged 65 to 74	5.11	41	4.3
Aged 75 or older	3.07	25	2.3

	AVERAGE HOUSEHOLD SPENDING	BEST CUSTOMERS (index)	BIGGEST CUSTOMERS (market share)
HOUSEHOLD INCOME			
Average household	**$12.44**	**100**	**100.0%**
Under $20,000	3.64	29	6.1
$20,000 to $39,999	9.47	76	16.9
$40,000 to $49,999	10.90	88	8.2
$50,000 to $69,999	5.73	46	7.0
$70,000 to $79,999	38.92	313	19.1
$80,000 to $99,999	18.71	150	12.5
$100,000 or more	20.44	164	29.4
HOUSEHOLD TYPE			
Average household	**12.44**	**100**	**100.0**
Married couples	15.92	128	64.9
Married couples, no children	13.98	112	25.0
Married couples, with children	19.57	157	38.8
Oldest child under age 6	5.15	41	1.8
Oldest child aged 6 to 17	13.87	111	14.3
Oldest child aged 18 or older	38.93	313	23.3
Single parent with child under age 18	24.37	196	11.3
Single person	6.91	56	16.1
RACE AND HISPANIC ORIGIN			
Average household	**12.44**	**100**	**100.0**
Asian	35.21	283	10.8
Black	2.16	17	2.1
Hispanic	4.17	34	3.9
Non-Hispanic white and other	15.21	122	93.4
REGION			
Average household	**12.44**	**100**	**100.0**
Northeast	19.52	157	29.0
Midwest	6.22	50	11.5
South	10.26	82	29.8
West	16.40	132	29.4
EDUCATION			
Average household	**12.44**	**100**	**100.0**
Less than high school graduate	2.61	21	3.1
High school graduate	8.04	65	16.5
Some college	11.04	89	19.4
Associate's degree	19.66	158	14.5
College graduate	19.94	160	46.4
Bachelor's degree	11.59	93	17.3
Master's, professional, doctoral degree	35.49	285	29.5

Note: Market shares may not sum to 100.0 because of rounding and missing categories by household type. "Asian" and "black" include Hispanics and non-Hispanics who identify themselves as being of the respective race alone. "Hispanic" includes people of any race who identify themselves as Hispanic. "Other" includes people who identify themselves as non-Hispanic and as Alaska Native, American Indian, Asian (who are also included in the Asian row), Native Hawaiian or other Pacific Islander, as well as non-Hispanics reporting more than one race.
Source: Calculations by New Strategist based on the Bureau of Labor Statistics' 2008 Consumer Expenditure Survey

Parking Fees and Tolls on Trips

Best customers:	Householders aged 45 to 64
	Married couples
	Asians and non-Hispanic whites
	Households in the Northeast
Customer trends:	Average household spending on parking fees and tolls on trips should rise as more boomers become empty-nesters and avid travelers—but only if discretionary income increases.

The most avid travelers spend the most on parking fees and tolls on trips. Householders aged 45 to 64 spend 29 to 34 percent more than average on this item. Married couples, with or without children at home, spend 42 percent more than average on parking fees and tolls on trips. Asian spending on this item is 22 percent above average, and non-Hispanic whites spend 15 percent more. Households in the Northeast spend 61 percent more than average on parking and tolls on trips because of the many toll roads in the region and the relatively high parking fees in congested Northeastern cities.

Average household spending on parking fees and tolls on trips rose 9 percent between 2000 and 2008, after adjusting for inflation. Average household spending on parking fees and tolls on trips should rise as more boomers become empty-nesters and avid travelers—but only if discretionary income increases.

Table 39. Parking fees and tolls on trips

Total household spending $1,249,969,500.00
Average household spends 10.35

	AVERAGE HOUSEHOLD SPENDING	BEST CUSTOMERS (index)	BIGGEST CUSTOMERS (market share)
AGE OF HOUSEHOLDER			
Average household	**$10.35**	**100**	**100.0%**
Under age 25	4.52	44	3.0
Aged 25 to 34	8.54	83	13.8
Aged 35 to 44	10.50	101	19.2
Aged 45 to 54	13.40	129	27.5
Aged 55 to 64	13.89	134	22.0
Aged 65 to 74	9.56	92	9.6
Aged 75 or older	5.38	52	4.9

	AVERAGE HOUSEHOLD SPENDING	BEST CUSTOMERS (index)	BIGGEST CUSTOMERS (market share)
HOUSEHOLD INCOME			
Average household	**$10.35**	**100**	**100.0%**
Under $20,000	2.29	22	4.6
$20,000 to $39,999	5.37	52	11.6
$40,000 to $49,999	5.68	55	5.1
$50,000 to $69,999	9.17	89	13.4
$70,000 to $79,999	12.00	116	7.1
$80,000 to $99,999	15.20	147	12.2
$100,000 or more	26.62	257	46.0
HOUSEHOLD TYPE			
Average household	**10.35**	**100**	**100.0**
Married couples	14.72	142	72.1
Married couples, no children	16.71	161	36.0
Married couples, with children	13.78	133	32.9
Oldest child under age 6	13.06	126	5.6
Oldest child aged 6 to 17	13.97	135	17.3
Oldest child aged 18 or older	13.89	134	10.0
Single parent with child under age 18	6.77	65	3.8
Single person	5.44	53	15.3
RACE AND HISPANIC ORIGIN			
Average household	**10.35**	**100**	**100.0**
Asian	12.60	122	4.6
Black	4.07	39	4.8
Hispanic	6.58	64	7.4
Non-Hispanic white and other	11.94	115	88.1
REGION			
Average household	**10.35**	**100**	**100.0**
Northeast	16.70	161	29.9
Midwest	9.21	89	20.5
South	8.55	83	29.9
West	9.18	89	19.8
EDUCATION			
Average household	**10.35**	**100**	**100.0**
Less than high school graduate	3.04	29	4.3
High school graduate	5.67	55	14.0
Some college	8.68	84	18.3
Associate's degree	9.05	87	8.0
College graduate	19.84	192	55.4
Bachelor's degree	15.55	150	27.9
Master's, professional, doctoral degree	27.53	266	27.5

Note: Market shares may not sum to 100.0 because of rounding and missing categories by household type. "Asian" and "black" include Hispanics and non-Hispanics who identify themselves as being of the respective race alone. "Hispanic" includes people of any race who identify themselves as Hispanic. "Other" includes people who identify themselves as non-Hispanic and as Alaska Native, American Indian, Asian (who are also included in the Asian row), Native Hawaiian or other Pacific Islander, as well as non-Hispanics reporting more than one race.
Source: Calculations by New Strategist based on the Bureau of Labor Statistics' 2008 Consumer Expenditure Survey

Recreational Expenses on Trips

Best customers:
  Householders aged 35 to 64
  Married couples without children at home
  Married couples with school-aged or older children at home
  Asians and non-Hispanic whites
  Households in the West

Customer trends:
  Average household spending on recreational expenses while traveling should grow as more boomers become empty-nesters and avid travelers, but only if discretionary income rises.

Recreational expenses on trips, the fifth largest travel expense, account for 9 percent of the average household's travel budget. The biggest spenders on recreational expenses on trips are middle-aged and older married couples. Householders ranging in age from 35 to 64 spend 19 to 34 percent more than average on this item. Married couples without children at home (most of them empty-nesters) spend 38 percent more than average on recreational expenses on trips, while those with school-aged or older children at home spend 52 to 73 percent more than average and control one-third of spending on this item. Asians, who have the highest incomes among ethnic and racial groups, spend 28 percent more than average on recreational expenses on trips. Non-Hispanic whites spend 15 percent more. Households in the West spend 35 percent more than average on this item.

Average household spending on recreational expenses on trips fell by a steep 26 percent between 2000 and 2008, after adjusting for inflation. Behind the decline was the economic downturn, which reduced spending on travel. Average household spending on recreational expenses while traveling should grow as more boomers become empty-nesters and avid travelers, but only if discretionary income rises.

Table 40. Recreational expenses on trips

Total household spending $16,229,072,600.00
Average household spends 134.38

	AVERAGE HOUSEHOLD SPENDING	BEST CUSTOMERS (index)	BIGGEST CUSTOMERS (market share)
AGE OF HOUSEHOLDER			
Average household	**$134.38**	**100**	**100.0%**
Under age 25	47.07	35	2.4
Aged 25 to 34	101.82	76	12.7
Aged 35 to 44	165.53	123	23.3
Aged 45 to 54	180.06	134	28.4
Aged 55 to 64	159.56	119	19.5
Aged 65 to 74	118.38	88	9.2
Aged 75 or older	64.41	48	4.6

	AVERAGE HOUSEHOLD SPENDING	BEST CUSTOMERS (index)	BIGGEST CUSTOMERS (market share)
HOUSEHOLD INCOME			
Average household	**$134.38**	**100**	**100.0%**
Under $20,000	33.72	25	5.3
$20,000 to $39,999	50.25	37	8.3
$40,000 to $49,999	79.77	59	5.5
$50,000 to $69,999	103.00	77	11.6
$70,000 to $79,999	133.34	99	6.0
$80,000 to $99,999	177.20	132	10.9
$100,000 or more	392.54	292	52.3
HOUSEHOLD TYPE			
Average household	**134.38**	**100**	**100.0**
Married couples	192.58	143	72.7
Married couples, no children	185.03	138	30.7
Married couples, with children	209.96	156	38.6
Oldest child under age 6	152.44	113	5.0
Oldest child aged 6 to 17	232.92	173	22.2
Oldest child aged 18 or older	204.59	152	11.3
Single parent with child under age 18	84.79	63	3.6
Single person	67.26	50	14.5
RACE AND HISPANIC ORIGIN			
Average household	**134.38**	**100**	**100.0**
Asian	172.43	128	4.9
Black	32.20	24	2.9
Hispanic	103.82	77	8.9
Non-Hispanic white and other	155.11	115	88.1
REGION			
Average household	**134.38**	**100**	**100.0**
Northeast	133.44	99	18.4
Midwest	128.25	95	22.0
South	110.03	82	29.6
West	180.98	135	30.0
EDUCATION			
Average household	**134.38**	**100**	**100.0**
Less than high school graduate	24.77	18	2.7
High school graduate	73.63	55	14.0
Some college	120.86	90	19.6
Associate's degree	127.23	95	8.7
College graduate	255.60	190	55.0
Bachelor's degree	201.36	150	27.8
Master's, professional, doctoral degree	352.95	263	27.2

Note: Market shares may not sum to 100.0 because of rounding and missing categories by household type. "Asian" and "black" include Hispanics and non-Hispanics who identify themselves as being of the respective race alone. "Hispanic" includes people of any race who identify themselves as Hispanic. "Other" includes people who identify themselves as non-Hispanic and as Alaska Native, American Indian, Asian (who are also included in the Asian row), Native Hawaiian or other Pacific Islander, as well as non-Hispanics reporting more than one race.
Source: Calculations by New Strategist based on the Bureau of Labor Statistics' 2008 Consumer Expenditure Survey

Restaurant and Carry-out Food on Trips

Best customers:	**Householders aged 45 to 64**
	Married couples without children at home
	Married couples with school-aged or older children at home
	Asians and non-Hispanic whites
Customer trends:	**Average household spending on restaurants while traveling should grow as boomers retire, but only if discretionary income rises.**

The biggest spenders on restaurant and carry-out meals on trips are the most avid travelers—older married couples. Householders aged 45 to 64 spend 27 to 40 percent more than average on this item. Married couples without children at home (most of them empty-nesters) spend 57 percent more than average on restaurant and carry-out meals on trips and control 35 percent of the market. Those with school-aged or older children at home spend 48 to 52 percent more. Asians, the most-affluent racial and ethnic group, spend 21 percent more than average on eating out while traveling. Non-Hispanic whites spend 17 percent more.

Average household spending on restaurant and carry-out meals on trips fell 12 percent between 2000 and 2008, after adjusting for inflation. Behind the decline was household budget cutting in the midst of the economic downturn. Spending on this item should grow in the years ahead as more boomers enter the best-customer lifestage, but only if discretionary income grows.

Table 41. Restaurant and carry-out food on trips

Total household spending	$28,727,559,900.00
Average household spends	237.87

	AVERAGE HOUSEHOLD SPENDING	BEST CUSTOMERS (index)	BIGGEST CUSTOMERS (market share)
AGE OF HOUSEHOLDER			
Average household	**$237.87**	**100**	**100.0%**
Under age 25	88.45	37	2.5
Aged 25 to 34	171.42	72	12.1
Aged 35 to 44	244.63	103	19.4
Aged 45 to 54	301.80	127	26.9
Aged 55 to 64	332.26	140	22.9
Aged 65 to 74	248.33	104	10.9
Aged 75 or older	131.37	55	5.3

	AVERAGE HOUSEHOLD SPENDING	BEST CUSTOMERS (index)	BIGGEST CUSTOMERS (market share)
HOUSEHOLD INCOME			
Average household	**$237.87**	**100**	**100.0%**
Under $20,000	65.06	27	5.7
$20,000 to $39,999	104.40	44	9.8
$40,000 to $49,999	149.71	63	5.9
$50,000 to $69,999	193.40	81	12.3
$70,000 to $79,999	252.11	106	6.5
$80,000 to $99,999	334.24	141	11.7
$100,000 or more	640.46	269	48.2
HOUSEHOLD TYPE			
Average household	**237.87**	**100**	**100.0**
Married couples	339.57	143	72.4
Married couples, no children	372.42	157	34.9
Married couples, with children	328.06	138	34.0
Oldest child under age 6	201.79	85	3.8
Oldest child aged 6 to 17	351.62	148	18.9
Oldest child aged 18 or older	362.58	152	11.3
Single parent with child under age 18	123.34	52	3.0
Single person	125.44	53	15.3
RACE AND HISPANIC ORIGIN			
Average household	**237.87**	**100**	**100.0**
Asian	288.05	121	4.6
Black	75.01	32	3.9
Hispanic	148.29	62	7.2
Non-Hispanic white and other	277.24	117	89.0
REGION			
Average household	**237.87**	**100**	**100.0**
Northeast	250.49	105	19.5
Midwest	223.35	94	21.6
South	199.16	84	30.3
West	305.15	128	28.6
EDUCATION			
Average household	**237.87**	**100**	**100.0**
Less than high school graduate	60.95	26	3.7
High school graduate	128.08	54	13.7
Some college	203.65	86	18.7
Associate's degree	241.11	101	9.3
College graduate	448.54	189	54.5
Bachelor's degree	360.17	151	28.1
Master's, professional, doctoral degree	607.13	255	26.4

Note: Market shares may not sum to 100.0 because of rounding and missing categories by household type. "Asian" and "black" include Hispanics and non-Hispanics who identify themselves as being of the respective race alone. "Hispanic" includes people of any race who identify themselves as Hispanic. "Other" includes people who identify themselves as non-Hispanic and as Alaska Native, American Indian, Asian (who are also included in the Asian row), Native Hawaiian or other Pacific Islander, as well as non-Hispanics reporting more than one race.
Source: Calculations by New Strategist based on the Bureau of Labor Statistics' 2008 Consumer Expenditure Survey

Ship Fares

Best customers:	**Householders aged 45 or older**
	Married couples without children at home
	Married couples with adult children at home
	Households in the West
	College graduates
Customer trends:	**Average household spending on ship fares will continue to increase as boomers fill the peak-spending lifestage—but only if discretionary income grows.**

The biggest spenders on ship fares are older Americans. Householders aged 45 to 64 spend 20 to 23 percent more than average on this item, while those aged 65 to 74 spend more than twice the average. Married couples without children at home (most of them empty-nesters) spend over two-and-one-half times the average on cruises and account for 58 percent of household spending on this item. Married couples with adult children at home spend 60 percent more than the average household on ship fares. College graduates, an affluent demographic group, spend twice the average on this item. Households in the West spend 50 percent more than average on ship fares.

Average household spending on ship fares declined 17 percent between 2000 and 2008, after adjusting for inflation. Behind the decline was the economic downturn, which reduced spending on travel. Average household spending on ship fares should increase in the years ahead as boomers fill the peak-spending lifestage—but only if discretionary income grows.

Table 42. Ship fares

Total household spending	$4,568,729,100.00
Average household spends	37.83

	AVERAGE HOUSEHOLD SPENDING	BEST CUSTOMERS (index)	BIGGEST CUSTOMERS (market share)
AGE OF HOUSEHOLDER			
Average household	**$37.83**	**100**	**100.0%**
Under age 25	6.01	16	1.1
Aged 25 to 34	15.63	41	6.9
Aged 35 to 44	24.01	63	12.0
Aged 45 to 54	45.26	120	25.4
Aged 55 to 64	46.39	123	20.1
Aged 65 to 74	84.50	223	23.3
Aged 75 or older	44.62	118	11.2

	AVERAGE HOUSEHOLD SPENDING	BEST CUSTOMERS (index)	BIGGEST CUSTOMERS (market share)
HOUSEHOLD INCOME			
Average household	**$37.83**	**100**	**100.0%**
Under $20,000	29.34	78	16.3
$20,000 to $39,999	14.29	38	8.4
$40,000 to $49,999	7.31	19	1.8
$50,000 to $69,999	22.62	60	9.1
$70,000 to $79,999	42.50	112	6.8
$80,000 to $99,999	38.50	102	8.4
$100,000 or more	103.95	275	49.2
HOUSEHOLD TYPE			
Average household	**37.83**	**100**	**100.0**
Married couples	61.02	161	81.8
Married couples, no children	97.68	258	57.6
Married couples, with children	32.06	85	20.9
Oldest child under age 6	8.90	24	1.0
Oldest child aged 6 to 17	23.61	62	8.0
Oldest child aged 18 or older	60.39	160	11.9
Single parent with child under age 18	11.06	29	1.7
Single person	14.04	37	10.8
RACE AND HISPANIC ORIGIN			
Average household	**37.83**	**100**	**100.0**
Asian	55.92	148	5.6
Black	8.26	22	2.7
Hispanic	10.26	27	3.1
Non-Hispanic white and other	46.70	123	94.3
REGION			
Average household	**37.83**	**100**	**100.0**
Northeast	38.63	102	18.9
Midwest	37.28	99	22.7
South	25.99	69	24.9
West	56.92	150	33.6
EDUCATION			
Average household	**37.83**	**100**	**100.0**
Less than high school graduate	7.46	20	2.9
High school graduate	21.68	57	14.6
Some college	25.41	67	14.7
Associate's degree	40.62	107	9.9
College graduate	75.84	200	58.0
Bachelor's degree	68.99	182	33.9
Master's, professional, doctoral degree	88.12	233	24.1

Note: Market shares may not sum to 100.0 because of rounding and missing categories by household type. "Asian" and "black" include Hispanics and non-Hispanics who identify themselves as being of the respective race alone. "Hispanic" includes people of any race who identify themselves as Hispanic. "Other" includes people who identify themselves as non-Hispanic and as Alaska Native, American Indian, Asian (who are also included in the Asian row), Native Hawaiian or other Pacific Islander, as well as non-Hispanics reporting more than one race.
Source: Calculations by New Strategist based on the Bureau of Labor Statistics' 2008 Consumer Expenditure Survey

Taxi Fares, Limousine Service, and Local Transportation on Trips

Best customers:	Householders aged 55 to 64 and 75 or older
	High-income households
	Married couples without children at home
	Married couples with adult children at home
	Asians
	Households in the Northeast and West
	College graduates
Customer trends:	Average household spending on local transportation on trips should rise as more boomers become empty-nesters and avid travelers, but only if discretionary income increases.

The most avid travelers spend the most on taxi fares, limousine services, and local transportation on trips. Householders aged 55 to 64 spend 44 percent more than average on this item, and householders aged 75 or older spend 37 percent more. Households with incomes of $100,000 or more spend three times the average on this item. Married couples without children at home (most of them empty-nesters) spend 59 percent more than average on taxi fares and local transportation on trips, while those with adult children at home spend 61 percent more than average. Asians spend one-third more than average on local transportation on trips. Households in the Northeast and West spend, respectively, 22 and 40 percent more than average on this item. College graduates spend more than twice the average on these services and control 60 percent of the market.

Average household spending on taxi fares, limousine services, and local transportation on trips declined 8 percent between 2000 and 2008, after adjusting for inflation. Average household spending on local transportation on trips should rise as more boomers become empty-nesters and avid travelers, but only if discretionary income increases.

Table 43. Taxi fares, limousine service, and local transportation on trips

Total household spending $2,359,845,800.00
Average household spends   19.54

	AVERAGE HOUSEHOLD SPENDING	BEST CUSTOMERS (index)	BIGGEST CUSTOMERS (market share)
AGE OF HOUSEHOLDER			
Average household	**$19.54**	**100**	**100.0%**
Under age 25	7.41	38	2.6
Aged 25 to 34	12.36	63	10.6
Aged 35 to 44	17.60	90	17.0
Aged 45 to 54	21.75	111	23.6
Aged 55 to 64	28.13	144	23.6
Aged 65 to 74	17.84	91	9.5
Aged 75 or older	26.79	137	13.0

	AVERAGE HOUSEHOLD SPENDING	BEST CUSTOMERS (index)	BIGGEST CUSTOMERS (market share)
HOUSEHOLD INCOME			
Average household	**$19.54**	**100**	**100.0%**
Under $20,000	3.54	18	3.8
$20,000 to $39,999	6.41	33	7.3
$40,000 to $49,999	9.60	49	4.6
$50,000 to $69,999	13.95	71	10.8
$70,000 to $79,999	21.20	108	6.6
$80,000 to $99,999	30.87	158	13.1
$100,000 or more	58.70	300	53.8
HOUSEHOLD TYPE			
Average household	**19.54**	**100**	**100.0**
Married couples	25.00	128	64.9
Married couples, no children	31.11	159	35.5
Married couples, with children	20.92	107	26.4
Oldest child under age 6	10.68	55	2.4
Oldest child aged 6 to 17	18.35	94	12.0
Oldest child aged 18 or older	31.44	161	12.0
Single parent with child under age 18	8.78	45	2.6
Single person	13.62	70	20.2
RACE AND HISPANIC ORIGIN			
Average household	**19.54**	**100**	**100.0**
Asian	25.76	132	5.0
Black	6.29	32	4.0
Hispanic	17.73	91	10.5
Non-Hispanic white and other	21.92	112	85.7
REGION			
Average household	**19.54**	**100**	**100.0**
Northeast	23.92	122	22.7
Midwest	15.02	77	17.7
South	15.35	79	28.4
West	27.35	140	31.2
EDUCATION			
Average household	**19.54**	**100**	**100.0**
Less than high school graduate	3.28	17	2.4
High school graduate	8.99	46	11.7
Some college	12.26	63	13.7
Associate's degree	25.83	132	12.1
College graduate	40.52	207	60.0
Bachelor's degree	29.46	151	28.0
Master's, professional, doctoral degree	60.38	309	32.0

Note: Market shares may not sum to 100.0 because of rounding and missing categories by household type. "Asian" and "black" include Hispanics and non-Hispanics who identify themselves as being of the respective race alone. "Hispanic" includes people of any race who identify themselves as Hispanic. "Other" includes people who identify themselves as non-Hispanic and as Alaska Native, American Indian, Asian (who are also included in the Asian row), Native Hawaiian or other Pacific Islander, as well as non-Hispanics reporting more than one race.
Source: Calculations by New Strategist based on the Bureau of Labor Statistics' 2008 Consumer Expenditure Survey

Train Fares, Intercity

Best customers: Householders aged 75 or older
Married couples without children at home
Married couples with adult children at home
Households in the Northeast and West
College graduates

Customer trends: Average household spending on train fares will continue to decline unless train
service improves.

Older Americans are the best customers of intercity train fares. Householders aged 75 or older spend 36 percent more than average on intercity train tickets. Married couples without children at home (most of them empty-nesters) spend 57 percent more than average on intercity train fares, while those with adult children at home spend 69 percent more than average. Households in the West spend 24 percent more than average on the train fares, while households in the Northeast spend 25 percent more. College graduates, who dominate the affluent, spend over twice the average on train travel.

Average household spending on intercity train fares fell 15 percent between 2000 and 2008, after adjusting for inflation. Behind the decline is the increasingly limited train service in the United States. Unless train service improves, average household spending on this item is likely to continue to decline.

Table 44. Train fares, intercity

Total household spending $2,700,417,200.00
Average household spends   22.36

	AVERAGE HOUSEHOLD SPENDING	BEST CUSTOMERS (index)	BIGGEST CUSTOMERS (market share)
AGE OF HOUSEHOLDER			
Average household	**$22.36**	**100**	**100.0%**
Under age 25	10.36	46	3.2
Aged 25 to 34	19.13	86	14.3
Aged 35 to 44	19.51	87	16.5
Aged 45 to 54	26.66	119	25.3
Aged 55 to 64	23.20	104	17.0
Aged 65 to 74	23.21	104	10.8
Aged 75 or older	30.35	136	12.9

	AVERAGE HOUSEHOLD SPENDING	BEST CUSTOMERS (index)	BIGGEST CUSTOMERS (market share)
HOUSEHOLD INCOME			
Average household	**$22.36**	**100**	**100.0%**
Under $20,000	5.00	22	4.7
$20,000 to $39,999	8.35	37	8.3
$40,000 to $49,999	10.25	46	4.3
$50,000 to $69,999	16.63	74	11.3
$70,000 to $79,999	38.51	172	10.5
$80,000 to $99,999	34.96	156	13.0
$100,000 or more	59.97	268	48.0
HOUSEHOLD TYPE			
Average household	**22.36**	**100**	**100.0**
Married couples	30.42	136	69.0
Married couples, no children	35.12	157	35.0
Married couples, with children	28.22	126	31.1
Oldest child under age 6	15.82	71	3.1
Oldest child aged 6 to 17	27.00	121	15.5
Oldest child aged 18 or older	37.70	169	12.5
Single parent with child under age 18	15.35	69	4.0
Single person	15.17	68	19.7
RACE AND HISPANIC ORIGIN			
Average household	**22.36**	**100**	**100.0**
Asian	27.62	124	4.7
Black	7.00	31	3.8
Hispanic	12.41	56	6.4
Non-Hispanic white and other	26.28	118	89.7
REGION			
Average household	**22.36**	**100**	**100.0**
Northeast	27.88	125	23.1
Midwest	23.26	104	23.9
South	15.68	70	25.4
West	27.70	124	27.6
EDUCATION			
Average household	**22.36**	**100**	**100.0**
Less than high school graduate	2.97	13	1.9
High school graduate	12.76	57	14.5
Some college	16.21	72	15.8
Associate's degree	17.58	79	7.2
College graduate	46.75	209	60.5
Bachelor's degree	34.60	155	28.7
Master's, professional, doctoral degree	68.55	307	31.7

Note: Market shares may not sum to 100.0 because of rounding and missing categories by household type. "Asian" and "black" include Hispanics and non-Hispanics who identify themselves as being of the respective race alone. "Hispanic" includes people of any race who identify themselves as Hispanic. "Other" includes people who identify themselves as non-Hispanic and as Alaska Native, American Indian, Asian (who are also included in the Asian row), Native Hawaiian or other Pacific Islander, as well as non-Hispanics reporting more than one race.
Source: Calculations by New Strategist based on the Bureau of Labor Statistics' 2008 Consumer Expenditure Survey

Vehicle Rentals on Trips

Best customers: **Householders aged 45 to 64**
                         High-income households
                         Married couples without children at home
                         Married couples with school-aged or older children at home
                         Asians and non-Hispanic whites
                         Households in the West
                         College graduates

Customer trends: **Average household spending on vehicle rentals on trips should grow in the years ahead as more boomers become empty-nesters and avid travelers, but only if discretionary income increases.**

The biggest spenders on rented vehicles while traveling are middle-aged and older married couples. Householders ranging in age from 45 to 64 spend 43 to 88 percent more than average on this item. Married couples without children at home (most of them empty-nesters) spend 57 percent more than average on vehicle rentals while traveling. Couples with school-aged or older children at home spend 29 to 83 percent more than average on this item. High-income households spend three times the average on vehicle rentals on trips. Asians spend 28 percent more than average, and non-Hispanic whites spend 16 percent more. Households in the West spend 60 percent more than average on vehicle rentals while traveling. College graduates spend more than twice the average on this item.

Average household spending on vehicle rentals while traveling declined by a steep 38 percent between 2000 and 2008, after adjusting for inflation. Price discounting was one factor behind the decline, as was the economic downturn. Average household spending on vehicle rentals while traveling should grow in the years ahead as more boomers become empty-nesters and avid travelers, but only if discretionary income increases.

Table 45. Vehicle rentals on trips

Total household spending $3,226,974,400.00
Average household spends   26.72

	AVERAGE HOUSEHOLD SPENDING	BEST CUSTOMERS (index)	BIGGEST CUSTOMERS (market share)
AGE OF HOUSEHOLDER			
Average household	**$26.72**	**100**	**100.0%**
Under age 25	4.23	16	1.1
Aged 25 to 34	19.38	73	12.1
Aged 35 to 44	21.70	81	15.4
Aged 45 to 54	38.32	143	30.4
Aged 55 to 64	50.29	188	30.9
Aged 65 to 74	19.77	74	7.7
Aged 75 or older	6.86	26	2.4

	AVERAGE HOUSEHOLD SPENDING	BEST CUSTOMERS (index)	BIGGEST CUSTOMERS (market share)
HOUSEHOLD INCOME			
Average household	**$26.72**	**100**	**100.0%**
Under $20,000	5.14	19	4.0
$20,000 to $39,999	11.85	44	9.9
$40,000 to $49,999	15.84	59	5.5
$50,000 to $69,999	21.00	79	11.9
$70,000 to $79,999	20.24	76	4.6
$80,000 to $99,999	31.52	118	9.8
$100,000 or more	81.15	304	54.4
HOUSEHOLD TYPE			
Average household	**26.72**	**100**	**100.0**
Married couples	37.42	140	71.0
Married couples, no children	41.96	157	35.0
Married couples, with children	37.78	141	34.9
Oldest child under age 6	28.35	106	4.7
Oldest child aged 6 to 17	34.60	129	16.6
Oldest child aged 18 or older	48.86	183	13.6
Single parent with child under age 18	10.99	41	2.4
Single person	15.63	58	17.0
RACE AND HISPANIC ORIGIN			
Average household	**26.72**	**100**	**100.0**
Asian	34.20	128	4.9
Black	12.06	45	5.5
Hispanic	13.80	52	6.0
Non-Hispanic white and other	31.02	116	88.6
REGION			
Average household	**26.72**	**100**	**100.0**
Northeast	25.93	97	18.0
Midwest	25.62	96	22.1
South	18.03	67	24.4
West	42.62	160	35.6
EDUCATION			
Average household	**26.72**	**100**	**100.0**
Less than high school graduate	4.47	17	2.4
High school graduate	13.98	52	13.3
Some college	15.40	58	12.6
Associate's degree	25.06	94	8.6
College graduate	58.25	218	63.0
Bachelor's degree	42.72	160	29.7
Master's, professional, doctoral degree	86.13	322	33.4

Note: Market shares may not sum to 100.0 because of rounding and missing categories by household type. "Asian" and "black" include Hispanics and non-Hispanics who identify themselves as being of the respective race alone. "Hispanic" includes people of any race who identify themselves as Hispanic. "Other" includes people who identify themselves as non-Hispanic and as Alaska Native, American Indian, Asian (who are also included in the Asian row), Native Hawaiian or other Pacific Islander, as well as non-Hispanics reporting more than one race.
Source: Calculations by New Strategist based on the Bureau of Labor Statistics' 2008 Consumer Expenditure Survey

Appendix: Spending by product and service, Ranked by amount spent, 2008

(average annual spending of consumer units on products and services, ranked by amount spent, 2008)

1.	Deductions for Social Security	$4,058.85
2.	Groceries (also shown by individual category)	3,744.50
3.	Mortgage interest (or rent, $2,615.04)	3,582.86
4.	Vehicle purchases (net outlay)	2,754.80
5.	Gasoline and motor oil	2,714.84
6.	Restaurants (also shown by meal category)	2,256.09
7.	Federal income taxes	1,817.03
8.	Property taxes	1,758.28
9.	Health insurance	1,653.37
10.	Electricity	1,353.35
11.	Vehicle insurance	1,113.37
12.	Dinner at restaurants	1,075.05
13.	Lunch at restaurants	772.73
14.	Cash contributions to church, religious organizations	744.52
15.	Vehicle maintenance and repairs	730.53
16.	College tuition	651.33
17.	Cellular phone service	642.57
18.	Maintenance and repair services, owner	629.92
19.	Deductions for private pensions	605.00
20.	Women's apparel	596.83
21.	Cable and satellite television services	583.58
22.	State and local income taxes	542.23
23.	Natural gas	531.24
24.	Nonpayroll deposit to retirement plans	524.48
25.	Residential telephone service and pay phones	467.06
26.	Alcoholic beverages	444.17
27.	Cash gifts to members of other households	409.13
28.	Prescription drugs	355.73
29.	Homeowner's insurance	354.07
30.	Men's apparel	344.17
31.	Airline fares	343.30
32.	Water and sewerage maintenance	332.13
33.	Lodging on trips	328.71
34.	Life and other personal insurance	316.83
35.	Vehicle finance charges	312.30
36.	Owned vacation homes	301.12
37.	Personal care services	291.13
38.	Cigarettes	284.01
39.	Dental services	254.54
40.	Day care centers, nurseries, and preschools	244.01
41.	Interest paid, home equity loan/line of credit	243.57
42.	Beef	238.87
43.	Restaurant meals on trips	237.87
44.	Leased vehicles	231.66
45.	Breakfast at restaurants	230.76
46.	Fresh fruits	221.93
47.	Computer information services	219.27
48.	Recreational vehicles (boats, campers, trailers)	218.05
49.	Other taxes	213.41
50.	Fresh vegetables	211.86
51.	Veterinarian services	206.96
52.	Elementary and high school tuition	190.11
53.	Child support expenditures	185.12
54.	Physician's services	182.11
55.	Finance charges, except mortgage and vehicles	179.99
56.	Snacks at restaurants	177.54
57.	Expenses for other properties	171.78
58.	Cash contributions to charities	168.83

59.	Television sets	$164.48
60.	Pet purchase, supplies, and medicines	164.01
61.	Movie, theater, amusement park, and other admissions	163.21
62.	Pet food	163.13
63.	Pork	162.98
64.	Poultry	159.05
65.	Computers and computer hardware for nonbusiness use	152.41
66.	Cosmetics, perfume, and bath products	151.17
67.	Fresh milk, all types	149.86
68.	Miscellaneous household products	147.91
69.	Laundry and cleaning supplies	147.82
70.	Prepared foods except frozen, salads, and desserts	144.42
71.	Legal fees	143.26
72.	Women's footwear	138.70
73.	Cheese	133.97
74.	Carbonated drinks	133.68
75.	Fish and seafood	127.88
76.	Social, recreation, civic club membership	127.49
77.	Household decorative items	126.77
78.	Toys, games, hobbies, and tricycles	122.55
79.	Beer and ale at home	122.12
80.	Girls' (aged 2 to 15) apparel	121.33
81.	Housekeeping services	118.86
82.	Fees for participant sports	117.48
83.	Gardening, lawn care service	115.65
84.	Fuel oil	115.45
85.	Trash and garbage collection	110.65
86.	Meats other than pork or beef	106.48
87.	Jewelry	105.23
88.	Support for college students	104.95
89.	Cleansing and toilet tissue, paper towels, and napkins	104.28
90.	Potato chips and other snacks	103.09
91.	Men's footwear	101.38
92.	Hospital room and services	101.09
93.	Fees for recreational lessons	99.44
94.	Lawn and garden supplies	98.04
95.	Vehicle registration	97.52
96.	Sofas	97.32
97.	Ready-to-eat and cooked cereals	93.88
98.	Children's (under age 2) apparel	92.72
99.	Deductions for government retirement	91.33
100.	Wine at home	87.56
101.	Nonprescription drugs	86.62
102.	Video game hardware and software	85.99
103.	Boys' (aged 2 to 15) apparel	82.71
104.	Babysitting and child care	82.33
105.	Stationery, stationery supplies, giftwrap	81.82
106.	Candy and chewing gum	80.02
107.	Lunch meats (cold cuts)	73.61
108.	Rent as pay	73.55
109.	Frozen meals	72.87
110.	Beer and ale at bars, restaurants	71.98
111.	Maintenance and repair materials, owner	71.07
112.	School lunches	70.84
113.	Postage	70.22
114.	Bedroom furniture except mattresses and springs	69.43
115.	Catered affairs	68.94
116.	Housing while attending school	68.44
117.	Hair care products	68.27
118.	Frozen prepared foods, except meals	67.72
119.	Lawn and garden equipment	65.40
120.	Bottled gas	64.07
121.	Bedroom linens	62.63
122.	Books and supplies for college	62.48
123.	Accounting fees	62.08

124.	Bread, other than white	$61.64
125.	Lottery and gambling losses	61.46
126.	Bottled water	61.35
127.	Admission to sports events	60.95
128.	Intracity mass transit fares	60.56
129.	Ice cream and related products	60.50
130.	Eyeglasses and contact lenses	59.90
131.	Canned and bottled fruit juice	58.82
132.	Funeral expenses	56.55
133.	Service by professionals other than physician	56.51
134.	Refrigerators and freezers	56.41
135.	Athletic gear, game tables, exercise equipment	56.41
136.	Books	55.23
137.	Sauces and gravies	54.33
138.	Professional laundry, dry cleaning	54.24
139.	Care for elderly, invalids, handicapped, etc.	53.92
140.	Lab tests, X-rays	53.64
141.	Mattresses and springs	52.42
142.	Eggs	51.06
143.	Coffee	50.95
144.	Ground rent	50.83
145.	Occupational expenses	50.65
146.	Other alcoholic beverages at bars, restaurants	50.30
147.	Property management, owner	50.20
148.	Biscuits and rolls	49.28
149.	Food prepared by consumer unit on trips	48.80
150.	Moving, storage, and freight express	47.32
151.	Cookies	46.85
152.	Indoor plants and fresh flowers	46.77
153.	Miscellaneous personal services	46.20
154.	Newspaper and magazine subscriptions	46.03
155.	Canned and packaged soups	45.81
156.	Cash contributions to educational institutions	45.52
157.	Wall units, cabinets, and other furniture	44.15
158.	Telephones and accessories	43.68
159.	Canned vegetables	42.89
160.	Coin-operated apparel laundry and dry cleaning	42.03
161.	Boys' footwear	41.00
162.	Cakes and cupcakes	40.13
163.	Alcoholic beverages purchased on trips	40.05
164.	Nonprescription vitamins	39.75
165.	Fats and oils	39.57
166.	Alimony expenditures	39.15
167.	Ship fares	37.83
168.	Nuts	37.40
169.	Parking fees	37.20
170.	White bread	36.96
171.	Pet services	36.77
172.	Rented vehicles	36.66
173.	Prepared salads	36.31
174.	Living room chairs	36.10
175.	Eye care services	35.98
176.	Wine at bars, restaurants	35.87
177.	Board (including at school)	35.03
178.	Crackers	34.99
179.	Kitchen and dining room furniture	34.82
180.	Washing machines	34.61
181.	Oral hygiene products	34.60
182.	Baby food	34.36
183.	Frozen vegetables	34.26
184.	Video cassettes, tapes, and discs	34.19
185.	Girls' footwear	33.36
186.	Outdoor equipment	32.72
187.	Hunting and fishing equipment	32.70
188.	Tea	32.13

189.	Deodorants, feminine hygiene, miscellaneous products	$32.10
190.	Cooking stoves, ovens	30.98
191.	Topicals and dressings	30.88
192.	Pasta, cornmeal, and other cereal products	30.59
193.	Photographer fees	30.45
194.	Musical instruments and accessories	30.12
195.	Tableware, nonelectric kitchenware	29.73
196.	Tobacco products other than cigarettes	29.35
197.	Salt, spices, and other seasonings	29.28
198.	Meals as pay	29.26
199.	Lamps and lighting fixtures	29.12
200.	Outdoor furniture	28.01
201.	Noncarbonated fruit-flavored drinks	27.98
202.	Photographic equipment	27.93
203.	Power tools	27.80
204.	Rental of video cassettes, tapes, discs, films	27.31
205.	Salad dressings	27.20
206.	Clothes dryers	27.04
207.	Wall-to-wall carpeting	26.99
208.	Frozen and refrigerated bakery products	26.10
209.	Baking needs	25.95
210.	Rice	25.32
211.	Jams, preserves, other sweets	25.05
212.	Other alcoholic beverages at home	24.84
213.	Computer software and accessories for nonbusiness use	23.57
214.	Recreation expenses on trips	23.55
215.	Closet and storage items	22.75
216.	Compact discs, records, and audio tapes	22.67
217.	Intercity train fares	22.36
218.	Bathroom linens	22.03
219.	Sweetrolls, coffee cakes, doughnuts	21.98
220.	Termite and pest control services	21.96
221.	Home security system service fee	21.75
222.	Sports drinks	21.60
223.	Gifts of stocks, bonds, and mutual funds to members of other households	21.42
224.	Checking accounts, other bank service charges	21.32
225.	Butter	21.28
226.	Window coverings	20.96
227.	Infants' equipment	20.87
228.	Curtains and draperies	20.75
229.	Canned fruits	20.55
230.	Frankfurters	20.51
231.	Cemetery lots, vaults, and maintenance fees	20.14
232.	Local transportation on trips	19.54
233.	Small electric kitchen appliances	19.36
234.	Tolls	18.98
235.	Shaving products	18.68
236.	Cream	18.26
237.	Care in convalescent or nursing home	18.23
238.	Fresh fruit juice	18.12
239.	Cash contributions to political organizations	17.89
240.	Automobile service clubs	17.79
241.	Appliance repair, including at service center	17.73
242.	Taxi fares and limousine service	17.71
243.	Sugar	17.68
244.	Floor coverings, nonpermanent	17.59
245.	Glassware	17.47
246.	Watches	17.43
247.	Living room tables	17.03
248.	Vocational and technical school tuition	17.02
249.	Books and supplies for elementary and high school	16.87
250.	Hand tools	16.70
251.	Camping equipment	16.66
252.	Nondairy cream and imitation milk	16.19
253.	Electric floor-cleaning equipment	16.04

254.	Laundry and cleaning equipment	$15.93
255.	Dishwashers (built-in), garbage disposals, range hoods	15.02
256.	School tuition other than college, vocational/technical, elementary, high school	14.95
257.	Satellite radio service	14.74
258.	Vegetable juices	14.72
259.	Pies, tarts, turnovers	14.71
260.	Maintenance and repair services, renter	14.55
261.	Newspapers and magazines, nonsubscription	14.45
262.	Nonalcoholic beverages (except carbonated, coffee, fruit-flavored drinks, and tea) and ice	14.28
263.	Bicycles	14.25
264.	Dried vegetables	14.15
265.	Nonelectric cookware	13.99
266.	Photo processing	13.93
267.	Personal digital audio players	13.56
268.	Portable heating and cooling equipment	13.55
269.	Olives, pickles, relishes	13.53
270.	Global positioning system devices	13.05
271.	Prepared desserts	13.03
272.	Hearing aids	12.91
273.	Peanut butter	12.83
274.	Luggage	12.44
275.	Lamb, organ meats, and others	12.35
276.	VCRs and video disc players	12.35
277.	Coal, wood, and other fuels	12.28
278.	Prepared flour mixes	11.88
279.	Whiskey at home	11.44
280.	Electric personal care appliances	11.43
281.	China and other dinnerware	11.13
282.	Intercity bus fares	11.07
283.	Tenant's insurance	11.03
284.	Phone cards	11.03
285.	Vehicle inspection	10.73
286.	Security services, owner	10.65
287.	Microwave ovens	10.52
288.	Sewing materials for household items	10.51
289.	Maintenance and repair materials, renter	10.29
290.	Sound equipment accessories	9.11
291.	Parking at owned home	8.94
292.	Margarine	8.67
293.	Deductions for railroad retirement	8.55
294.	Rental of party supplies for catered affairs	8.39
295.	Infants' furniture	8.37
296.	Flour	7.92
297.	Office furniture for home use	7.84
298.	Sound components and component systems	7.81
299.	Dried fruits	7.58
300.	Shopping club membership fees	7.56
301.	Driver's license	7.44
302.	Live entertainment for catered affairs	7.33
303.	Material for making clothes	7.29
304.	Vacation clubs	7.28
305.	Repairs and rentals of lawn and garden equipment, hand and power tools, etc.	7.03
306.	Repair of computer systems for nonbusiness use	6.67
307.	Artificial sweeteners	6.48
308.	Docking and landing fees	6.46
309.	Apparel alteration, repair, and tailoring services	6.39
310.	Kitchen and dining room linens	6.22
311.	Voice over IP	6.18
312.	Reupholstering and furniture repair	6.11
313.	Hair accessories	5.99
314.	Sewing patterns and notions	5.81
315.	Frozen fruit juices	5.68
316.	Frozen fruits	5.64
317.	Streamed and downloaded audio	5.47

318.	Playground equipment	$5.44
319.	Watch and jewelry repair	5.15
320.	Sewing machines	5.09
321.	Window air conditioners	5.02
322.	Rental of recreational vehicles	5.01
323.	Miscellaneous video equipment	4.90
324.	Water-softening service	4.89
325.	Stamp and coin collecting	4.74
326.	Bread and cracker products	4.71
327.	Towing charges	4.61
328.	Medical equipment for general use	4.22
329.	Delivery services	4.19
330.	Repair of TV, radio, and sound equipment	3.78
331.	Safe deposit box rental	3.73
332.	Tape recorders and players	3.63
333.	Flatware	3.62
334.	Nonclothing laundry and dry cleaning, coin-operated	3.37
335.	Water sports equipment	3.32
336.	Smoking accessories	3.31
337.	Septic tank cleaning	3.24
338.	Film	2.99
339.	Slipcovers and decorative pillows	2.93
340.	Rental and repair of miscellaneous sports equipment	2.90
341.	Supportive and convalescent medical equipment	2.88
342.	Internet services away from home	2.87
343.	Plastic dinnerware	2.83
344.	Personal digital assistants	2.81
345.	Radios	2.81
346.	Winter sports equipment	2.62
347.	Books and supplies for vocational and technical schools	2.62
348.	Rental of furniture	2.44
349.	Wigs and hairpieces	2.40
350.	Business equipment for home use	2.27
351.	Clothing rental	2.22
352.	Global positioning services	2.11
353.	Online gaming services	2.02
354.	Credit card memberships	1.70
355.	Rental and repair of musical instruments	1.67
356.	Rental of medical equipment	1.60
357.	Fireworks	1.55
358.	Pinball, electronic video games	1.50
359.	Satellite dishes	1.48
360.	Clothing storage	1.44
361.	Rental of supportive and convalescent medical equipment	1.39
362.	Shoe repair and other shoe services	1.27
363.	Smoke alarms	1.22
364.	Other serving pieces	1.21
365.	Streamed and downloaded video	1.12
366.	Nonclothing laundry and dry cleaning, sent out	1.10
367.	Installation of television sets	1.03
368.	Portable dishwashers	0.97
369.	Appliance rental	0.92
370.	Repair and rental of photographic equipment	0.74
371.	School bus	0.70
372.	Rental of television sets	0.62
373.	Books and supplies for day care and nursery	0.53
374.	Installation of computer	0.47
375.	Telephone answering devices	0.44
376.	Rental of VCR, radio, and sound equipment	0.39
377.	Dating services	0.26
378.	Rental of computer and video game hardware and software	0.20

Source: Calculations by New Strategist based on the 2008 Consumer Expenditure Survey

Glossary

age The age of the reference person.

alcoholic beverages Includes beer and ale, wine, whiskey, gin, vodka, rum, and other alcoholic beverages.

annual spending The annual amount spent per household. The Bureau of Labor Statistics calculates the annual average for all households in a segment, not just for those that purchased an item. The averages are calculated by integrating the results of the diary (weekly) and interview (quarterly) portions of the Consumer Expenditure Survey. For items purchased by most households—such as bread—average annual spending figures are a fairly accurate account of actual spending. For products and services purchased by few households during a year's time—such as cars—the average annual amount spent is much less than what purchasers spend.

apparel, accessories, and related services Includes the following:
* *men's and boys' apparel* Includes coats, jackets, sweaters, vests, sport coats, tailored jackets, slacks, shorts and short sets, sportswear, shirts, underwear, nightwear, hosiery, uniforms, and other accessories.
* *women's and girls' apparel* Includes coats, jackets, furs, sport coats, tailored jackets, sweaters, vests, blouses, shirts, dresses, dungarees, culottes, slacks, shorts, sportswear, underwear, nightwear, uniforms, hosiery, and other accessories.
* *infants' apparel* Includes coats, jackets, snowsuits, underwear, diapers, dresses, crawlers, sleeping garments, hosiery, footwear, and other accessories for children.
* *footwear* Includes articles such as shoes, slippers, boots, and other similar items. It excludes footwear for babies and footwear used for sports such as bowling or golf shoes.
* *other apparel products and services* Includes material for making clothes, shoe repair, alterations and sewing patterns and notions, clothing rental, clothing storage, dry cleaning, sent-out laundry, watches, jewelry, and repairs to watches and jewelry.

baby boom Americans born between 1946 and 1964.

cash contributions Includes cash contributed to persons or organizations outside the consumer unit including court-ordered alimony, child support payments, and support for college students, and contributions to religious, educational, charitable, or political organizations.

consumer unit (1) All members of a household who are related by blood, marriage, adoption, or other legal arrangements; (2) a person living alone or sharing a household with others or living as a roomer in a private home or lodging house or in permanent living quarters in a hotel or motel, but who is financially independent; or (3) two or more persons living together who pool their income to make joint expenditure decisions. Financial independence is determined by the three major expense categories: housing, food, and other living expenses. To be considered financially independent, at least two of the three major expense categories have to be provided by the respondent. For convenience, called household in the text of this report.

consumer unit, composition of The classification of interview households by type according to (1) relationship of other household members to the reference person; (2) age of the children of the reference person; and (3) combination of relationship to the reference person and age of the children. Stepchildren and adopted children are included with the reference person's own children.

earner A consumer unit member aged 14 or older who worked at least one week during the twelve months prior to the interview date.

education Includes tuition, fees, books, supplies, and equipment for public and private nursery schools, elementary and high schools, colleges and universities, and other schools.

entertainment Includes the following:
* *fees and admissions* Includes fees for participant sports; admissions to sporting events, movies, concerts, plays; health, swimming, tennis, and country club memberships, and other social recreational and fraternal organizations; recreational lessons or instructions; and recreational expenses on trips.
* *audio and visual equipment and services* Includes television sets; radios; cable TV; tape recorders and players; video cassettes, tapes, and discs; video cassette recorders and video disc players; video game hardware and software; personal digital audio players; streaming and downloading audio and video; sound components; CDs, records, and tapes; musical instruments; and rental and repair of TV and sound equipment.
* *pets, toys, hobbies, and playground equipment* Includes pet food, pet services, veterinary expenses, toys, games, hobbies, and playground equipment.
* *other entertainment equipment and services* Includes indoor exercise equipment, athletic shoes, bicycles, trailers, campers, camping equipment, rental of cameras and trailers, hunting and fishing equipment, sports equipment, winter sports equipment, water sports equipment, boats, boat motors and boat trailers, rental of boats, landing and docking fees, rental and repair of sports equipment, photographic equipment, film, photo processing, photographer fees, repair and rental of photo equipment, fireworks, pinball and electronic video games.

expenditure The transaction cost including excise and sales taxes of goods and services acquired during the survey period. The full cost of each purchase is recorded even though full payment may not have been made at the date of purchase. Expenditure estimates include gifts. Excluded from expenditures are purchases or portions of purchases directly assignable to business purposes and periodic credit or installment payments on goods and services already acquired.

federal income tax Includes federal income tax withheld in the survey year to pay for income earned in survey year plus additional tax paid in survey year to cover any underpayment or underwithholding of tax in the year prior to the survey.

financial products and services Includes accounting fees, legal fees, union dues, professional dues and fees, other occupational expenses, funerals, cemetery lots, dating services, shopping club memberships, and unclassified fees and personal services.

food Includes the following:
* *food at home* Refers to the total expenditures for food at grocery stores or other food stores during the interview period. It is calculated by multiplying the number of visits to a grocery or other food store by the average amount spent per visit. It excludes the purchase of nonfood items.
* *food away from home* Includes all meals (breakfast, lunch, brunch, and dinner) at restaurants, carry-outs, and vending machines, including tips, plus meals as pay, special catered affairs such as weddings, bar mitzvahs, and confirmations, and meals away from home on trips.

generation X Americans born between 1965 and 1976; also known as the baby-bust generation.

gifts for people in other households Includes gift expenditures for people living in other consumer units. The amount spent on gifts is also included in individual product and service categories.

health care Includes the following:

• *health insurance* Includes health maintenance plans (HMOs), Blue Cross/Blue Shield, commercial health insurance, Medicare, Medicare supplemental insurance, long-term care insurance, and other health insurance.

• *medical services* Includes hospital room and services, physicians' services, services of a practitioner other than a physician, eye and dental care, lab tests, X-rays, nursing, therapy services, care in convalescent or nursing home, and other medical care.

• *drugs* Includes prescription and nonprescription drugs, internal and respiratory over-the-counter drugs.

• *medical supplies* Includes eyeglasses and contact lenses, topicals and dressings, antiseptics, bandages, cotton, first aid kits, contraceptives; medical equipment for general use such as syringes, ice bags, thermometers, vaporizers, heating pads; supportive or convalescent medical equipment such as hearing aids, braces, canes, crutches, and walkers.

Hispanic origin The self-identified Hispanic origin of the consumer unit reference person. All consumer units are included in one of two Hispanic origin groups based on the reference person's Hispanic origin: Hispanic or non-Hispanic. Hispanics may be of any race.

household According to the Census Bureau, all the people who occupy a household. A group of unrelated people who share a housing unit as roommates or unmarried partners is also counted as a household. Households do not include group quarters such as college dormitories, prisons, or nursing homes. A household may contain more than one consumer unit. The terms household and consumer unit are used interchangeably in this report.

household furnishings and equipment Includes the following:

• *household textiles* Includes bathroom, kitchen, dining room, and other linens, curtains and drapes, slipcovers and decorative pillows, and sewing materials.

• *furniture* Includes living room, dining room, kitchen, bedroom, nursery, porch, lawn, and other outdoor furniture.

• *carpet, rugs, and other floor coverings* Includes installation and replacement of wall-to-wall carpets, room-size rugs, and other soft floor coverings.

• *major appliances* Includes refrigerators, freezers, dishwashers, stoves, ovens, garbage disposals, vacuum cleaners, microwave ovens, air-conditioners, sewing machines, washing machines, clothes dryers, and floor-cleaning equipment.

• *small appliances and miscellaneous housewares* Includes small electrical kitchen appliances, portable heating and cooling equipment, china and other dinnerware, flatware, glassware, silver and other serving pieces, nonelectric cookware, and plastic dinnerware. Excludes personal care appliances.

• *miscellaneous household equipment* Includes computer hardware and software, luggage, lamps and other lighting fixtures, window coverings, clocks, lawn mowers and gardening equipment, hand and power tools, telephone answering devices, personal digital assistants, Internet services away from home, office equipment for home use, fresh flowers and house plants, rental of furniture, closet and storage items, household decorative items, infants' equipment, outdoor equipment, smoke alarms, other household appliances, and small miscellaneous furnishing.

household services Includes the following:

• *personal services* Includes baby sitting, day care, and care of elderly and handicapped persons.

• *other household services* Includes computer information services; housekeeping services; gardening and lawn care services; coin-operated laundry and dry-cleaning of household textiles; termite and pest control products; moving, storage, and freight expenses; repair of household appliances and other household equipment; reupholstering and furniture repair; rental and repair of lawn and gardening tools; and rental of other household equipment.

housekeeping supplies Includes soaps, detergents, other laundry cleaning products, cleansing and toilet tissue, paper towels, napkins, and miscellaneous household products; lawn and garden supplies, postage, stationery, stationery supplies, and gift wrap.

housing tenure Owner includes households living in their own homes, cooperatives, condominiums, or townhouses. Renter includes households paying rent as well as families living rent free in lieu of wages.

income before taxes The total money earnings and selected money receipts accruing to a consumer unit during the 12 months prior to the interview date. Income includes the following components:

• *wages and salaries* Includes total money earnings for all members of the consumer unit aged 14 or older from all jobs, including civilian wages and salaries, Armed Forces pay and allowances, piece-rate payments, commissions, tips, National Guard or Reserve pay (received for training periods), and cash bonuses before deductions for taxes, pensions, union dues, etc.

• *self-employment income* Includes net business and farm income, which consists of net income (gross receipts minus operating expenses) from a profession or unincorporated business or from the operation of a farm by an owner, tenant, or sharecropper. If the business or farm is a partnership, only an appropriate share of net income is recorded. Losses are also recorded.

• *Social Security, private and government retirement* Includes payments by the federal government made under retirement, survivor, and disability insurance programs to retired persons, dependents of deceased insured workers, or to disabled workers; and private pensions or retirement benefits received by retired persons or their survivors, either directly or through an insurance company.

• *interest, dividends, rental income, and other property income* Includes interest income on savings or bonds; payments made by a corporation to its stockholders, periodic receipts from estates or trust funds; net income or loss from the rental of property, real estate, or farms, and net income or loss from roomers or boarders.

• *unemployment and workers' compensation and veterans' benefits* Includes income from unemployment compensation and workers' compensation, and veterans' payments including educational benefits, but excluding military retirement.

• *public assistance, supplemental security income, and food stamps* Includes public assistance or welfare, including money received from job training grants; supplemental security income paid by federal, state, and local welfare agencies to low-income persons who are aged 65 or older, blind, or disabled; and the value of food stamps obtained.

• *regular contributions for support* Includes alimony and child support as well as any regular contributions from persons outside the consumer unit.

• *other income* Includes money income from care of foster children, cash scholarships, fellowships, or stipends not based on working; and meals and rent as pay.

indexed spending Indexed spending figures compare the spending of particular demographic segments with that of the average household. To compute an index, the amount spent on an item by a demographic segment is divided by the amount spent on the item by the average household. That figure is then multiplied by 100. An index of 100 is the average for all households. An index of 132 means average spending by households in a segment is 32 percent above average (100 plus 32). An index of 75 means average spending by households in a segment is 25 percent below average (100 minus 25). Indexed spending figures identify the consumer units that spend the most on a product or service.

life and other personal insurance Includes premiums from whole life and term insurance; endowments; income and other life insurance; mortgage guarantee insurance; mortgage life insurance; premiums for personal life liability, accident and disability; and other non–health insurance other than homes and vehicles.

market share The market share is the percentage of total household spending on an item that is accounted for by a demographic segment. Market shares are calculated by dividing a demographic segment's total spending on an item by the total spending of all households on the item. Total spending on an item for all households is calculated by multiplying average spending by the total number of households. Total spending on an item for each demographic segment is calculated by multiplying the segment's average spending by the number of households in the segment. Market shares reveal the demographic segments that account for the largest share of spending on a product or service.

millennial generation Americans born between 1977 and 1994.

occupation The occupation in which the reference person received the most earnings during the survey period. The occupational categories follow those of the Census of Population. Categories shown in the tables include the following:

• *self-employed* Includes all occupational categories; the reference person is self-employed in own business, professional practice, or farm.

• *wage and salary earners, managers and professionals* Includes executives, administrators, managers, and professional specialties such as architects, engineers, natural and social scientists, lawyers, teachers, writers, health diagnosis and treatment workers, entertainers, and athletes.

• *wage and salary earners, technical, sales, and clerical workers* Includes technicians and related support workers; sales representatives, sales workers, cashiers, and sales-related occupations; and administrative support, including clerical.

• *retired* People who did not work either full- or part-time during the survey period.

owner S*ee* housing tenure.

pensions and Social Security Includes all Social Security contributions paid by employees; employees' contributions to railroad retirement, government retirement and private pensions programs; retirement programs for self-employed.

personal care Includes products for the hair, oral hygiene products, shaving needs, cosmetics, bath products, suntan lotions, hand creams, electric personal care appliances, incontinence products, other personal care products, personal care services such as hair care services (haircuts, bleaching, tinting, coloring, conditioning treatments, permanents, press, and curls), styling and other services for wigs and hairpieces, body massages or slenderizing treatments, facials, manicures, pedicures, shaves, electrolysis.

quarterly spending Quarterly spending data are collected in the interview portion of the Consumer Expenditure Survey. The quarterly spending tables show the percentage of households that purchased an item during an average quarter, and the amount spent during the quarter on the item by purchasers. Not all items are included in the interview portion of the Consumer Expenditure Survey.

reading Includes subscriptions for newspapers, magazines, and books through book clubs; purchase of single-copy newspapers and magazines, books, and encyclopedias and other reference books.

reference person The first member mentioned by the respondent when asked to Start with the name of the person or one of the persons who owns or rents the home. It is with respect to this person that the relationship of other consumer unit members is determined. Also called the householder or head of household.

region Consumer units are classified according to their address at the time of their participation in the survey. The four major census regions of the United States are the following state groupings:

• *Northeast* Connecticut, Maine, Massachusetts, New Hampshire, New Jersey, New York, Pennsylvania, Rhode Island, and Vermont.

• *Midwest* Illinois, Indiana, Iowa, Kansas, Michigan, Minnesota, Mississippi, Nebraska, North Dakota, Ohio, South Dakota, and Wisconsin.

• *South* Alabama, Arkansas, Delaware, District of Columbia, Florida, Georgia, Kentucky, Louisiana, Maryland, Mississippi, North Carolina, Oklahoma, South Carolina, Tennessee, Texas, Virginia, and West Virginia.

• *West* Alaska, Arizona, California, Colorado, Hawaii, Idaho, Minnesota, Nevada, New Mexico, Oregon, Utah, Washington, and Wyoming.

renter S*ee* housing tenure.

shelter Includes the following:

• *owned dwellings* Includes interest on mortgages, property taxes and insurance, refinancing and prepayment charges, ground rent, expenses for property management and security, homeowner's insurance, fire insurance and extended coverage, landscaping expenses for repairs and maintenance contracted out (including periodic maintenance and service contracts), and expenses of materials for owner-performed repairs and maintenance for dwellings used or maintained by the consumer unit, but not dwellings maintained for business or rent.

• *rented dwellings* Includes rent paid for dwellings, rent received as pay, parking fees, maintenance, and other expenses.

• *other lodging* Includes all expenses for vacation homes, school, college, hotels, motels, cottages, trailer camps, and other lodging while out of town.

• *utilities, fuels, and public services* Includes natural gas, electricity, fuel oil, coal, bottled gas, wood, other fuels; residential telephone service, cell phone service, phone cards; water, garbage, trash collection; sewerage maintenance, septic tank cleaning; and other public services.

size of consumer unit The number of people whose usual place of residence at the time of the interview is in the consumer unit.

state and local income taxes Includes state and local income taxes withheld in the survey year to pay for income earned in survey year plus additional taxes paid in the survey year to cover any underpayment or underwithholding of taxes in the year prior to the survey.

tobacco and smoking supplies Includes cigarettes, cigars, snuff, loose smoking tobacco, chewing tobacco, and smoking accessories such as cigarette or cigar holders, pipes, flints, lighters, pipe cleaners, and other smoking products and accessories.

transportation Includes the following:

• *vehicle purchases (net outlay)* Includes the net outlay (purchase price minus trade-in value) on new and used domestic and imported cars and trucks and other vehicles, including motorcycles and private planes.

• *gasoline and motor oil* Includes gasoline, diesel fuel, and motor oil.

• *other vehicle expenses* Includes vehicle finance charges, maintenance and repairs, vehicle insurance, and vehicle rental licenses and other charges.

• *vehicle finance charges* Includes the dollar amount of interest paid for a loan contracted for the purchase of vehicles described above.

• *maintenance and repairs* Includes tires, batteries, tubes, lubrication, filters, coolant, additives, brake and transmission fluids, oil change, brake adjustment and repair, front-end alignment, wheel balancing, steering repair, shock absorber replacement, clutch and transmission repair, electrical system repair, repair to cooling system, drive train repair, drive shaft and rear-end repair, tire repair, vehicle video equipment, other maintenance and services, and auto repair policies.

• *vehicle insurance* Includes the premium paid for insuring cars, trucks, and other vehicles.

• *vehicle rental, licenses, and other charges* Includes leased and rented cars, trucks, motorcycles, and aircraft, inspection fees, state and local registration, drivers' license fees, parking fees, towing charges, tolls on trips, and global positioning services.

• *public transportation* Includes fares for mass transit, buses, trains, airlines, taxis, private school buses, and fares paid on trips for trains, boats, taxis, buses, and trains.

weekly spending Weekly spending data are collected in the diary portion of the Consumer Expenditure Survey. The data show the percentage of households that purchased an item during the average week, and the amount spent per week on the item by purchasers. Not all items are included in the diary portion of the Consumer Expenditure Survey.